ENRIQUE OLVERA

SUNNY DAYS TACO NIGHTS

WITH ALONSO RUVALCABA

PHOTOGRAPHS BY ARACELI PAZ

LEGEND

VEGETARIAN

VEGAN

v

NUT-FREE

DAIRY-FREE

GLUTEN-FREE

5 INGREDIENTS OR FEWER

-5

30 MINUTES OR LESS

-30

PREFACE

When I was at culinary school in New York, in the late 1990s, New American cuisine—fusion-type cooking that embraces global cuisines and seasonal ingredients—was in full swing. This movement was led by chefs Thomas Keller, Larry Forgione, Alice Waters, and many others. As a Mexican, I felt it natural to think that this movement could be replicated in my own country. I believed that Mexico's extensive and deep culinary tradition would make such a thing not only possible but also relatively easy to achieve.

However, it had not yet happened. Likely, the term "contemporary Mexican cuisine" had not even entered the conversation. Most Mexican chefs at the time did not dare experiment with traditional recipes, and the attempts made by a few of us weren't always well received. Granted, many of those first attempts were far from brilliant, and most did not stand the test of time. But we knew that within traditional recipes, which had been so intensely preserved from generation to generation, there was the potential for new ways of adding to our gastronomic heritage.

We tried to establish new conversations within our cuisine. Our ideas came from a place of admiration and respect, and we were convinced that there were (and are) countless possibilities of what can be created—not only in terms of dishes but also in their execution and presentation. Our legacy will be innovation through experimentation and learning from our history—from what has been tried, tested, and repeated over and over again, across generations.

I was born and raised in Mexico City. My family was middle class, and the daily cooking at home would not be classified as traditional, though my mother did make *pipián* and *entomatado* from time to time. On our table, you were more likely to see carrot cream or veal Milanese.

My professional training was in classical European techniques, and when I opened my first restaurant, Pujol, in 2000, I did not feel confident enough with traditional Mexican recipes to propose modern versions. Instead, we served haute cuisine. However, I felt most comfortable with street food, since it was part of my childhood: I remember the *esquite* stand outside the bakery, selling corn salad; the chicharrón stand in the park; and the fried quesadillas and cakes sold outside my school. Mexicans love to eat on the street!

My restaurant struggled to attract customers, and I knew that street vendors never had that problem. In 2004, I began adding more traditional dishes, such as *robalito al pastor* and quesadilla, to the menu. Their almost immediate success was a clear sign. The first "tacos" at Pujol were not prepared in the traditional way; rather, they were dishes that *evoked* tacos. It was during my first visit to Japan, that I understood that the respect for the taco could be similar to that for sushi: that a popular dish, enjoyed by all classes, could be offered in different contexts and prepared with varying degrees of rigor and complexity.

At Pujol, the kitchen's first experiments with tacos began only after we had been open for over a decade. We started by making flavored tortillas using, for example, chiles, and by using other foods in place of tortillas. After a couple of years, as we continued our exploration, we realized it was also important to delve deeper into the quality of the ingredients, and to perfect our techniques. We began on a somewhat purist path, laying the foundation for our deeper understanding of and appreciation for the corn we worked with. We recognized and defended the value of conserving our native corn, while remaining aware of the importance of this grain as the basis of the diet of millions of Mexicans. We decided to give the grain the place it deserves, and treat it as an authentic specialty product, like wine and coffee. We began to recognize the origin and qualities of each variety of tortilla—the characteristics of each dough, and therefore of the tortillas they produce, and ultimately of the tacos created using it.

Tacos are versatile both in their ingredients and in the contexts in which they are presented, not only at a local level but even at an international level. Each day the making of tacos allows us to make small discoveries. It's this daily, creative process that helps ensure the permanence of the taco.

ENRIQUE OLVERA

DISCOVERIES

Like a virus spreading through the air or like death itself, the taco is the great equalizer, the greatest of equalizers. If the taco is the great equalizer that brings us all together, regardless of how we identify as men or women, then the taco, like death, is without prejudice. This is evident. No tricycle, bike, truck, or taco cart will explicitly say it, but none of them denies or excludes; they never refuse their service to anyone based on nationality, language, sex, age, disability, social status, indigenous identity, gender identity, physical appearance, health condition, religion, thoughts, orientation, sexual preference, or tattoos, or for any other reason. The taco is the opposite of exclusive: it is genuinely for the masses—not just in words or a damn sign, but for real. For everyone.

The taco is a knife that cuts vertically through the layers of the city. These layers can be socio-economic, gender-related, or geopolitical—it doesn't matter; the taco will pierce through them. Like an earthquake, the taco disregards the geopolitical lines of cities. There is no city district, neighborhood, or local constituency without several taquerías in the form of food establishments or semi-fixed or mobile stalls. (By the way, movement is an endearing characteristic of the taquería. The taco is on the run: you have to chase it through the city.) Like an earthquake, the taco also ignores the schedules of daily life. Or it knows them but doesn't care: all hours are taco hours. There are tacos that tend to the morning, like basket tacos—a classic order is one with beans and green salsa, one with pork cracklings and pickled strips, and one with adobo with both toppings . . . but I'll talk about sauces in a moment; there are tacos that tend to noon—two examples are carnitas and battered fish; there are tacos that feel more comfortable during the night.

TACO NIGHT

I repeat: there is no such thing as a taco hour. All tacos can shine at any time. The movement of the taco is like the movement we perceive of the sun around the earth: just as deceptive, just as false. In reality, the taco is like the sun—we move around its bare-bulb spotlight on the socket hanging from the roof of a humble room. The taco is still, and we invent hours around it.

And behold, we have decided that one of the taco hours is the late-night–early morning hour: the last hour of each day. After the oratory of the west, comes the sermon of three in the morning. (Someone else might say that this hour is not the last but the first hour of the day. And they would be right. Right now, 3 AM is the last and darkest hour in Mexico City, Los Angeles, Tijuana, and New York City, and it's also their first hour. The taco night has one foot in Friday and another in Saturday, touching both days at the same time.)

What do we seek in this borderline hour? We can understand only one thing in the semi-alcoholic mist of a party among friends: the body needs food, and it needs that food to be very greasy. It's biological. When our body lacks nutrients, we crave the most energy-dense foods, meaning heat and calories: fats. But we want those fats to have something that sharpens them: lemon acidity, the sweet spiciness of chile morita. We seek the finicky edge of onion, the fresh grassy flavor of cilantro (coriander); we seek this spring or summerlike, tropical, peaceful thing called pineapple. In five words: we seek tacos al pastor. The al pastor taco is the vampire taco. It is the taco that never sleeps (and never dies either). It seems to start in the early morning; it is there at ten in the morning; it's the noon sun; it takes a little break at five in the afternoon, then gets ready to serve us dinner at eight in the evening; and its ever-firm spit is our north again at three in the morning. The al pastor taco is also endlessly linked to the exit from the cinema and other shows. After a movie event like Barbenheimer: let's go for some al pastor, right? After a Taylor Swift concert: let's go for some al pastor, right? The taco is like a compass that moves us through time and space in cities.

And we go to it on taco night, but we don't go alone; we experience it as communion or a ritual. Or like a cult that is not violent but friendly. It doesn't have to be al pastor. In other places, they go for shawarmas or kebabs. In our cities, we can go for suadero tacos, arab tacos, charcoal-grilled tacos, head tacos, "cochinada" tacos, suckling pig taco in Oaxaca de Juárez, grilled beef taco in Tijuana, Baja California. We toast with a taco—sometimes we even say cheers—because the taco is the Nosferatu food: the taco is the undead.

ABOUT THE ROLE OF TACOS

In large cities, like Mexico City or Los Angeles, the taco has a doubly regional character: it belongs to its neighborhood and to a region of the country. Among these regions are, like moving mirrors, Mexico City or Los Angeles themselves. As we know, there are purely "chilango" tacos and completely "Angelino" ones. The taco is the symbol of the city of migrations.

There are, of course, Michoacán carnitas tacos, Veracruz minilla tacos, Baja California fish tacos, Toluca bishop tacos, Yucatán *cochinita* tacos, Oaxacan suckling pig tacos, Pueblan Arab tacos, "chilango" suadero tacos, Hidalguenese *barbacoa* tacos, Sonoran grilled beef tacos, Sinaloan golden tacos. Then there are Korean tacos and Chinatown neighborhood tacos and Chinese tacos (which are not the same) and Thai tacos, and Argentine chorizo tacos, and so on endlessly. Endlessly.

The taco is the symbol of the city because it also symbolizes the triumph of migration over our innate xenophobia: the triumph of equity over our inherited inequality. The taco is a lingua franca, we all speak it whether we want to or not, and we all understand it.

Now, the taco extends its domain. Today's taco is not yesterday's, and it will not be tomorrow's. Today's taco, for example, has moved (temporarily) to the restaurant. Perhaps you are too young to remember this, but in the past when our ancestors ruled the land, the taco was street food. It was food to eat while standing or, with much effort, sitting on white or red plastic stools with their Coca-Cola signs.

Mom, Dad, and my siblings would go on Thursdays after watching a movie, and we would stand in front of the charcoal grill at "Los Parados" (one example among thousands: everyone has their neighborhood taquería), which was not a restaurant but a charcoal grill. We would eat pork chops and steak with lemon and pico de gallo or "pebre" or Mexican salsa, or whatever you call it. If someone brought out a stool for the lady, well, thank you very much, sir.

But like the universe or the shape of your face, the taco is always changing. The taco entered the restaurant, and very thoughtful minds have explored it, changed it, and happily intellectualized it to make it what it is now: a quest for technical perfection, wit, and engineering. Yet something remains of the standing taco, the gritty sidewalk taco with the occasional rat keeping an eye out and twitching its pink or gray nose to see what it can capture if the city's rodent luck favors it.

There is a struggle between the street, the home, and the restaurant. There are tacos that have not entered the restaurant—truly standing tacos, eaten barely under the occasional blue umbrella held up by a plastic table.

They are the last frontier of sidewalk tacos—for example, basket tacos (and the most sidewalk-oriented among basket tacos are the ones set up outside high schools and universities). There are bar tacos and home tacos; there are tacos that cannot live outside the fine-dining restaurant. There is an even more sidewalk-oriented, more hardworking taco, a solitary collective taco. We eat it standing when there's no other choice, but generally, we eat it sitting on a little stool, on a planter, or just on the curb. It's the tortilleria taco. It's as cheap as a compliment or an insult. We all know a tortilleria or several. (Molino "El Pujol" is the gentrified version of all of them.) The tortilleria kitchen has achieved one of the ultimate goals of the ideal restaurant: consistency—that is, stability, solidity, the ability to repeat a dish without any changes whatsoever: no mistakes, no improvements. And so, we go and buy, we the people without a future or the people who know that our only certain future is today.

The tortilleria taco is persistently humble: it possesses the virtue of understanding its own limitations and weaknesses and acts accordingly. The tortilleria taco is heartbreakingly humble.

(By the way, there is no more domestic taco than the salted taco that Mom rolls with a hand movement and hands to her son or daughter as soon as they leave the tortilla line. Anyone who doesn't catch that reference has missed a life of love and tenderness.)

In this book, you will find all the forms of these tacos.

TOWARDS THE FINAL POINT (OF THE BEGINNING)

The taco renews itself insistently. "The taco is a way of life," said chef Enrique Olvera, owner of one of the best taquerías in Mexico. Perhaps he means that the life of a human being (Mexican) eventually adapts to geography, climate, and language, and produces a taco. No matter where, the taco seeks to be born, like those flowers that suddenly sprout between the cracks of a wall or on an unlikely sidewalk. "The taco is a way of eating," others say. Perhaps they mean that the taco is looking for food around it to attract and turn into a taco. If the taco is a way of eating, anything edible is susceptible to becoming a taco.

One can be more precise: the taco is not a way of eating but a model, or a template, of a way of eating. In this model, the intelligence and creativity of countless cooks' work contribute to the intellectual renewal of this "way of eating," creating a constant base to work from.

How does this intellectual renewal happen? It can be through recontextualization—moving a taco from its "natural element" to place it in a foreign space, for

example, as happened in Pujol around the year 2010. (Today, the appearance of a *barbacoa* taco in the city's most expensive restaurant seems the most normal thing in the world, or even a bit outdated.) It can also be through rethinking, or reimagining, as in the case of tacos that are not tacos but only seem like tacos or remind us of them. They are not visibly tacos but possess "taquitud," that essential quality of being a taco. It can also be through play, challenge, nostalgic memory, or parody. The taco renews itself insistently. The taco is in the brain, not on the plate. The taco is a cell that explodes.

HISTORICAL NOTES

No one knows, nor will anyone ever know, who ate the first taco or what they wanted to name it. One author suggests that there were already "carnitas in taco, with hot tortillas" at Hernán Cortés' triumphant banquet in the village of Coyoacán. H. M. Romero proposes that the word taco derives from "itacate," which is a bundle of food for taking away. It would be very convenient and charming if the taco had been born with the first mixing in Mexico (corn and pork!) and that its name had Nahuatl origins. The truth, as far as we know, is that the taco and the word "taco" advanced on separate and slowly converging lines for several centuries. From its creation the tortilla was probably used to wrap other foods, and the signifier "taco" gradually approached this meaning.

Antoine Oudin translated "taco" into French in 1607 as "la bourre dequoy on charge les arquebuses ou pistoles," meaning "the wad with which muskets or pistols are loaded." Taco also meant a peg to tighten something (Covarrubias, 1611), a stick for playing billiards or tricks (Stevens in 1706: "A Tack to Play at Billiards"), and a carpenter's hammer. The *Diccionario de Autoridades* (1739) adds this curious definition: "Among drinkers, they call the sips of wine, which they drink after eating: and so they say, Let's throw four tacos." By the mid-nineteenth century, Ramón Joaquín Domínguez could note (in *Diccionario nacional*) that "taco" meant "Snack that is taken [...] outside meal hours, and so we say: have a taco." In the Escenas Andaluzas, there is this phrase: "Take this taco and this drink." Here, the taco is a tapa or a snack. Something of the form (wad) and something of the context (the tavern) bring those tacos closer to "our" taco.

These scenes are from 1847. Even by that year, the "taco" had not appeared in any Mexican context. Melchor Ocampo had not included the word in his vernacular compendium *Idiotismos hispano-mexicanos* (1844), where "mole" and "tamal" appear, and it is not in *El Cocinero Mexicano* (1831), where there are quesadillas de ahuatle, chalupas de morcón, and tlataoyos rellenos, which are wrapped in *pipián*, or wrapped in Nana Rosa. Nana Rosas, says the *El Cocinero Mexicano*, "are filled with scrambled eggs or minced meat, and on top, they are adorned with sliced onion, chili peppers, olives, almonds quartered, raisins, pine nuts, pieces of candied citron, and strands of fried meat or lean ham, also fried." Read them carefully after almost two centuries, and Nana Rosa's wraps are almost tacos.

The lines of "taco" the dish and "taco" the word finally touch in a satirical poem from 1862. It is one of the instances of poetry against gluttons. It is also a mockery of Juan Nepomuseno Almonte, who gave a grand banquet to the French generals Frédéric Forey and M. Dubois de Saligny. (It's the year of the French invasion, remember—the one we celebrate on May 5.) In the poem, Almonte calls Forey "tehutli," "god". No one comes out well from here:

The Teutil Forey
Was with us happily,
He ate pipián, and tamali,
Temolito with xumiles,
And he indulged of mextapiles
In his tlaxcalli tacos.

"Tacos de tlaxcalli" is equivalent to saying "tortilla tacos." The specification may imply that the word "taco" wasn't necessarily associated with tortillas; that was a younger meaning. Even in "Los bandidos de Río Frío," almost thirty years after that poem, Manuel Payno describes a moment at a feast for the Virgin of Guadalupe like this:

Most families, outdoors, forming cheerful groups and with a devouring appetite, tearing off the tasty fragments of a roasted goat leg with their teeth; and the kids jumping around with their tortilla tacos with avocado in hand.

Today, of course, those tacos would simply be avocado tacos.

At the end of the nineteenth century, taquerías already existed in Mexico City. Some were just a basket with sweaty tacos (or "miner tacos," as they were called). Others, a brazier at a door, almost like a shelter. Beatriz Muciño Reyes had one like that on Cadena Street, which we now call Venustiano Carranza; she later moved it to what is now Bolívar, and finally, in 1907, to Uruguay Street. Beatriz continued serving tacos there until 1945. In 2008, Tacos Beatriz had to close. The twentieth century was a bad century for everyone. A few taquerías were in the courtyard of the neighborhood and also served as dining spaces for families. The custom persists.

Like Beatriz, there were many female *taqueras* at the beginning. Most came from outside, including Beatriz from San Mateo Tazcaliatac and Esther Torres from Guanajuato. There were taquerías specializing in Jalisco, Toluca, and Veracruz styles. The taquerías contributed to migration. Someone, without approval, wrote in 1920 that Paseo de la Alameda was a "provincial affair": Oaxacan chocolates, dishes from Guadalajara, sweets from Morelia. The art of the taquería allowed for an excursion, and a kind of culinary tourism for those who couldn't afford a trip.

The taquería was also a safety net against unemployment. Daytime taquerías, which generally sold tacos with vegetarian stews or chicken, were run by women while the men took on other work. (Doña Beatriz closed at five o'clock.) Nighttime taquerías, with their inclination towards drinking and commotion, sold tacos with offal meats or pork rinds and were attended by men, while the women of the house fed the children or performed other tasks assigned to them by the accursed patriarchy. The distinction continues. Are there women who tend to *pastor* spits or suadero cauldrons at midnight? Are there men who prepare tlacoyos in the morning? The traditional taquería is a conservative space—a space that needs to be breached. Restaurants like Pujol or Damián are breaking it open. This is the beginning of the middle of the twenty-first century.

Here, have a little salted taco before you go.

Where is the taco right now? In 2011, Pujol—undoubtedly the best restaurant in Mexico City at that time—proposed a completely taco-centric menu. Later, in 2017, it designed an omakase of tacos for its bar. (The omakase remains.) Today, there's hardly a single "fine dining" restaurant in Mexico that doesn't have at least one taco on its menu.

The gentrification or refinement or embourgeoisement of the taco might seem like a relatively recent phenomenon, but the truth is that since it began to rise in popularity in the first half of the twentieth century, decent people have sought to adapt it to their elegant tables. There is embourgeoisement by substitution. As early as 1903, *El Diario del Hogar* featured paradoxical "taquitos de harina" made not with nixtamal dough but with a wheat flour, butter, cream, and baking powder mixture, covered with sugar and cinnamon. In the same newspaper, in 1908, there were "tacos de crema" that actually called for French crepes. ("It is filled with milk dessert, cream, or some dried preserve, and rolled like a taco.") The plebeian taco transforms, with this French appearance, into an aristocratic taco. It's the same substitution that some restaurants have practiced for decades with their huitlacoche crepes, or in many middle-class homes, by making "ham tacos," where the meat replaces the tortilla.

There is embourgeoisement through ornamentation. El Diario del Hogar, in the twenties, recommended that "tacos de crema" be placed on the platter in the form of a pyramid, covered with egg white icing, and adorned with strawberries and orange and violet flowers. The tactic of decorating (and refining) with flowers immediately refers to the so-called "new Mexican cuisine" and its proliferation of rose petals and the current custom of adorning the bourgeois taco with cilantro, borage, or nasturtium flowers.

There is also embourgeoisement through inaccessibility. Toward the late fifties, engineer Alfonso Gándara created a mold to make tortillas that dispensed with traditional presses and, armed with his invention, installed hundreds of tortilla shops across the country. Suddenly, the craft of making tortillas by hand was seen as laborious and worthy of attention. Some snobbish restaurants of the time made it very visible that they hired tortilla makers to make tortillas by hand on clay comals. In some restaurants, you can still see this slightly touristy curiosity.

More than the torta, more than the tamale, more than any other dish we can imagine as "Mexican," the taco is always advancing. It adopts the fickle customs of its consumers—"techno-emotional" cuisine, the "return to the ingredient," "gastronomic nationalism"—it changes, clings, or becomes almost unrecognizable. The taco is a work in progress.

ALONSO RUVALCABA

OUR TACOS

ASADA TACOS

Before tacos, before the history of cooking, before Homo sapiens, there was grilling, its history going back to the domestication of fire by Homo erectus during the Stone Age. Putting grilled meat into a tortilla, into a cooked *masat*, is a much more recent idea, and marks one of the peaks of human intelligence. Every minute, no matter the time zone, somewhere in Mexico meat is being grilled over fire, to be used in a taco. In the smoky corridors of Oaxaca, there's a butcher right now placing sliced meat on irons, and someone else ready to sell their sauces. In the immense restaurants of Monterrey, young goats, skewered on sticks, are leaning over hot coals—this is called *pastor*-style goat there. At a stall in Tijuana, someone is adding a hefty spoonful of mashed avocado to their grilled meat taco; in Barra Vieja, near Acapulco, someone is adding beans and grilled fish to a whitish tortilla; in Guasave, Sinaloa, another is sobering up with the first tacos of roast pork, seared on both sides before dawn—they come in flour tortillas and with a lot of "flag" sauce, as it's known there (a mix of chopped tomato, onion, and serrano chile; others call it Mexican sauce; yet others, pico de gallo); at a market in Mexico City, someone is ordering Argentine chorizo in tacos, and it's doused with lime juice and chimichurri. Everyone will go home with a smile on their face and the distinct smell of char clinging to their clothes.

BAJO TIERRA

The first ovens were underground—given the tools at hand, it was easier to dig than to build. Indigenous people in Mexico roasted meats in pits, and those pits, covered with mud, sticks, branches, and leaves, were called some variation of the word "barbecue." The beautiful method of cooking underground continues to this day, and many of those cooking ingredients end up in a taco. In central Mexico, what was once the heart of the country's pulque production (pulque is a fermented alcoholic drink made from the leaves of maguey, a type of agave), lambs with their stomachs filled with entrails are baked underground, wrapped in maguey leaves that have been softened by the fire for a few seconds. In the north—on the borders with Texas, New Mexico, and Arizona—under the earth, large cow heads are also baked in maguey leaves. Their cheeks are then chopped into tiny pieces and placed in flour tortillas, then served with lemon and piquín chile sauce. In the Yucatán, sunbathed by the tremendous yellow sun, pigs and chickens and turkeys are rubbed with achiote and other seasonings, then wrapped and baked in banana leaves.

CAPEADOS

Tacos capeados, lightly battered and deep-fried, were long viewed by Mexicans as a guilty pleasure. Today, the pleasure we derive from a taco of Veracruz-style battered fish fillet or, in Baja California, a Rosarito-style battered shrimp (prawn) taco—with its cabbage and mysterious white sauce—is an antidote to guilt. The same can be said of tacos with very lightly breaded charales or other small fish—in the style of Michoacán and the Altiplano Lake area. In Mexico City, the great family of *tacos capeados* can be divided into three groups: *tortitas capeadas*, *chiles capeados*, and *milanesos*. The *tortitas* must include *quelites*, tender edible greens, kneaded with egg and then breaded and deep-fried, as well as potato and beef. Almost always filled with cheese, *chiles capeados*—battered chile tacos—are a beautiful example of vegetarian street food. *Milanesos*—battered meat tacos— are becoming increasingly bulky and more imaginative: there is beef, pork, chicken; there is breaded ham, and breaded pork and cheese; there is cheese or ham. All are bathed in a delicious sauce. And there is also *campechano*—a *milanesa* filled with stew. Would you like it with beans or with rice? Have it with a little of both to make it a complete meal.

CONFIT

Into the great cauldron of the world, the primal copper pot—that convex contraption where liquid accumulates around the edges and a plate shines in the center—a *taquera* or *taquero* deposits and heats lard over medium heat. They then place pieces of meat in it and cook them rapidly. This is not deep-frying, though it *is* frying and it *is* deep. Rather, it's confiting—letting the fat penetrate the meat, letting the meat infuse the fat. Meat and fat exchange their essences, they get to know each other and create a friendship that will soon be impossible to undo, and whose expression will be the taco. The pork carnitas taco is perhaps the most refined example, whether in the style of Michoacán—in a large tortilla, unpressed—or in the chilango style—in a small *taquera* tortilla, passed through the grill (griddle). Carnitas are also a triumph of a taco: the belly is a pork belly squared by the human hand; the *bofe* is the lung; the *buche*, the stomach; the *nana* is the uterus; the *moño*, the intestines; the *nenepil*, the belly combined with the uterus. Knowing carnitas is a way of knowing Spanish. From beef, the suadero and the tripe are confited, and both, after the confit and before the tortilla, pass through the sausage-maker's grill. It is common to emphasize when ordering tripe, "Golden brown, please." (It's best that way.) The *cochinada* taco—made with leftovers accumulated at the edges of the sausage-maker's grill: sausage, suadero, crackling, confit—can be seen as the quintessence of this genre of taco. Its flavor lasts several days and nights at the back of the mouth.

DORADOS/ FLAUTAS/ HARD SHELL

This, unlike the confit tacos, are indeed deep-fried: it's a quick frying of the entire taco. The crispy taco from a local eatery is usually made with chicken or potato, topped with a salad of lettuce, onion, and tomato, and almost always fresh salsa. The *flauta* from a *flautería* tends to be beef topped with cream and fresh cheese. There's room for crossover with the deep-fried taco—it can be found at various types of venues throughout Mexico: a good lamb barbecue stand in the Altiplano area will offer taco *dorado*; every Michoacán carnitas stand will serve a folded and fried taco filled with pig brains cleverly called *sesadilla*; seafood restaurants tend to serve fried shrimp (prawn) or fish folded tacos (*pescadillas*!); and in some taco shops in Mexico City, you'll find crispy *pastor* tacos—but without the pineapple. The *taco dorado* covers all genres and styles. The *taco dorado* welcomes you.

GUISADOS

A stew taco is the culmination of culinary ingenuity and resourcefulness. Let's say that three dishes exist and lead their separate lives, and that red rice is one of those dishes, refried beans is another, and the third is pork cracklings in green sauce. They were made yesterday or the day before, each served separately. Today is a day or two or three later, and each of these dishes converges with the others into a new dish: the stew taco. This can be the combination of several dishes and a form of remix and translation: of taking one thing from where it was to new places. The stew taco is the working taco, the mobile taco, chasing the crowd through the city: it arrives in a van or on a tricycle at the farthest back corner of the highest point of the hill, or at the fence surrounding the construction site, to wait for the lunch hour. Or sometimes, as with the first taco vendors in the city, stew tacos come out through a gate with simply a grill (griddle) and some pots. A stew taco is a complete meal: the tortillas, the rice or beans, and the stew. It's a symbol of both our poverty and our haste.

HORNO

Is a roasted chicken taco an oven taco? The roasted pork taco, especially the Oaxaca style or those from Hispanic-Mexican restaurants—like the ones at Casino Español in downtown Mexico City—are definitely oven-made, sometimes very juicy, sometimes leaning toward crispy. Jalisco-style birria is cooked in an oven at high heat, around 400°F/200°C, and then it's finished off quickly in a very hot oven, as high as it can go. In the classic sandwich shops of Mexico City, like Casa del Pavo, Rey del Pavo, and La Rambla—all established in the early twentieth century—oven-roasted turkey is briefly grilled and served on a corn tortilla, sometimes lightly moistened with fat or broth. (You have to ask for it.) Practically everything can be prepared in an oven, but a baked pork leg in marinade, the meat served on a corn tortilla with a few shreds of red onion, should be considered one of the great achievements of Mexican cuisine.

PLANCHA

Let's talk about the grill (griddle) tacos. The *gaonera*, made of delicate beef steaks, is the simplest and juiciest taco made on the grill: it's simply a steak barely moistened with its own juices. The *gaonera* is inspired by Rodolfo Gaona, master of the bullring in the early 1900s. There is a tradition of grill tacos associated with bullfighting. Villamelón-style tacos—named after a type of fair-weather bullfighting enthusiast—tend to be made of finely chopped and grilled steak. They can also be made of *campechanos*, a mix of *cecina* and longaniza sausage, or of *cecina* with longaniza, pork cracklings, and *chile cuaresmeño* (also called *costeños*). Taco sellers on tricycles carrying a grill park at busy corners of Mexico City, where they sell steak, longaniza, *campechanos*, and *alambre* tacos—a brilliant mix of steak, bacon, peppers, and onion. They are often accompanied by french fries. In every city in Mexico, there are stalls selling liver tacos with onions—grilled quickly, sometimes with sliced serranoes. In Mexico State, in central Mexico, tacos of charcuterie are also made on the grill. These are made of *obispo*, a casing filled with viscera somewhat reminiscent of haggis; of *queso de puerco*, or head cheese, packed in a *tompiate*, a kind of braided palm basket; of *cecina*, barely dried and lightly salted meat; and of various chorizos—with flavored almonds, green or slightly yellow from the habanero. Taco carts and tricycles with grills offer a sauce made of various chiles and tomatoes crushed in a *molcajete* (a Mexican mortar and pestle) and then roasted. The containers holding the *salsa madre*, which thickens as it sits, are replenished throughout the day.

TROMPO

The *trompo* taco is probably the most recognizably Mexican taco. The *trompo* taco is as important as a Mexican museum or library. In this taco, the history of migrations, the waning moon of the Ottoman Empire, the arrival of immigrants from Lebanon and their adaptation to local livestock and local adobos, and the influence of geography on a dish are all visible. It might have been the first taco made in the world. A *trompo* is a vertical rotating spit. Spit roasting is probably the first ever cooking method, and as soon as there was cooked dough, someone likely filled it with roasted meat! While roasted meat was at first cooked horizontally on a spit, it likely wasn't long before it was being stacked vertically, to take advantage of gravity to allow all those delicious meat juices to drip down onto the lower layers.

The *trompo* taco arrived in Mexico perhaps as shawarma, kebab, gyro—all of which survive in regional kitchens— and then it was adapted. As it moved from Lebanon to Yucatán to Puebla to Mexico City and shed the Islamic tradition of lamb, it began to be made of pork, seasoned with chiles, and flavored with pineapple. In many places, its unleavened bread was replaced by corn tortillas. Then cheese was added and placed between two wheat flour tortillas. We call the *trompo* taco *gringa*, a name loaded with folk etymology and legend. In Tijuana, the *trompo* taco, also fondly known around the world as *al pastor* taco, is called *adobada*. The *trompo* taco is a sign of friendship and the endless links that connect one human being with all the others. In Puebla, some taquerías have two *trompos* facing the street: one flesh-colored, one reddish, both heated by charcoal, one for Arab tacos, the other for "CDMX-style" tacos.

VAPOR

Some historians say that the first taco sold in Mexico City was the *taco de canasta* or "sweaty" taco. Perhaps they are right: the convenience of selling tacos from a large basket that turns into a steamer, and where the stacking and enclosure improve the taste of the taco throughout the morning, is obvious.

In Guadalajara, steamed tacos usually come not in a basket but in a pot, though the principle of accumulating sweat through stacking is the same, as is the case with *olla*-style tacos in Monclova, a city in northern Mexico. The morning tacos in Monterrey—made from *cabeza* or *barbacoa*—are steamed but not stacked. In convenience stores in Texas, breakfast tacos are wrapped in a kind of aluminum that takes advantage of the taco's own steam to keep it warm and comforting. The beef-head tacos in Mexico City stay hot thanks to the steam from a covered *baño maría* of sorts, the meat and tortillas kept separate until serving time. And what is a *mixiote* if not meat—beef, chicken, even fish—steamed enclosed in a thin piece of maguey leaf, which is then wrapped in a tortilla that's also been steamed? Season with lime, white onion, and manzano chile, and you'll have a classic steamed taco from the pulque region of central Mexico.

TACOS AL CARBÓN

Prep time: 30 minutes , plus 1 hour
marinating time
Cooking time: 7 minutes
Makes: 8

For the beef ribs:
• ½ white onion, diced
• 2 cloves garlic
• Scant ½ cup (3½ fl oz/100 ml)
  vegetable oil
• 6 black peppercorns, toasted
• 4 cloves, toasted
• ½ teaspoon ground oregano, toasted
• ¼ teaspoon salt
• Juice of 3 lemons
• 10½ oz/300 g boneless beef ribs
• 3 teaspoons olive oil, for greasing

To serve:
• 8 Corn Tortillas (page 200)
• Lime wedges
• Your choice of sauces (pages 184–97)

One must think of this taco as a stimulus for the imagination. Here we specify using boneless beef ribs, but any self-respecting *taquera* or *taquero* will also have in their repertoire chicken breast, thin pork chop, skirt steak, and perhaps *nopal*—prickly pear. The options are many and worthy of exploration for this taco.

It is essential to use a charcoal grill, to give the taco its unique flavor.

FOR THE BEEF RIBS
Put all the ingredients except the ribs into a blender and blend into a smooth paste. Transfer the paste to a bowl, add the ribs and coat well with the paste. Refrigerate for 1 hour to marinate.

Preheat a charcoal grill (barbecue) to medium. Brush with the olive oil, then place the ribs on the grill and cook for 2 minutes on each side or until browned. Remove and cut into strips.

TO SERVE
Place the tortillas on the grill, flipping them continuously for 2–3 minutes or until warmed through. Transfer the tortillas to a plate and serve alongside the beef, lime wedges, and any of our sauces.

SMOKED BEEF TACOS

Cooking time: 5 minutes, plus 2 hours
smoking time
Makes: 4

For the meat:
- Smoking wood, such as oak or walnut
- 1 cup (8 oz/225 g) salt
- 1 cup (4¼ oz/120 g) black pepper
- 2 lb 4 oz/1 kg beef brisket, trimmed

To serve:
- 4 Corn Tortillas (page 200)
- Pico de Gallo (page 191)
- Cilantro (coriander) leaves, stems removed
- Lime wedges

This taco has gained popularity especially in certain areas of Mexico and the United States where backyard grilling is common. It's important to have a grill or smoker with a lid, so the smoke doesn't escape.

FOR THE MEAT
Put the smoking wood in a smoker or grill (barbecue) with a lid and preheat to 250°F/120°C. Meanwhile, combine the salt and black pepper in a bowl. Massage the brisket with the seasoning, ensuring it's thoroughly covered. Place the meat in the smoker (with the fattiest part facing down) and smoke for 2 hours. Remove the meat from the smoker and thinly slice.

TO SERVE
Heat a skillet over high heat for 5 minutes. Add the tortillas in pairs, flipping them continuously until warmed through. Transfer to a fabric napkin to keep them warm. Then, transfer to the plate, top with the smoked beef slices, and then with the pico de gallo and cilantro (coriander). Serve with lime wedges on the side.

ARGENTINIAN TACOS

● ● ❦ -30

Prep time: 10 minutes
Cooking time: 7 minutes
Makes: 4

- 1 tablespoon salt
- 1 tablespoon black pepper
- ½ tablespoon garlic powder
- 4 × 10½ oz/300 g Argentinian beef steaks

To serve:
- 4 Corn Tortillas (page 200)
- 4 lime wedges
- Your choice of sauces (pages 184–97)

This is a typical taco from the *tianguis*—*tianguis* is a Nahuatl word meaning "open-air markets"—of Mexico City, which are popular on Saturdays. Of course, you can make it on your Sunday barbecue day too. If you have Chimichurri (page 186) on hand, please use it here.

Preheat a grill (griddle) over medium heat for 15 minutes.

In a medium bowl, combine the salt, pepper, and garlic powder. Season the steaks generously with the season-ing, covering both sides. Place on the grill and cook for 2½ minutes on each side for medium-well. To check for the doneness of the meat, pierce the center with a metal skewer—the more resistance there is, the rarer it is.

TO SERVE
Heat a skillet over high heat for 5 minutes. Add the tortillas, flipping them continuously for 2–3 minutes or until warmed through.

Place the meat on a plate, slice it, and serve with tortillas, lime wedges, and any of our sauces on the side.

SONORA-STYLE CARNE ASADA TACOS

TACOS DE CARNE
ASADA ESTILO
SONORENSE

Prep time: 30 minutes
Cooking time: 40 minutes
Makes: 4

- 4 potatoes
- 4 tablespoons butter
- 3½ oz/100 g crispy bacon
- 4 tablespoons finely chopped parsley leaves
- 2 lb 4 oz/1 kg sirloin steak
- Salt
- Black pepper

To serve:
- 4 Flour Tortillas (page 201)
- Lime wedges

This is a taco to enjoy at an afternoon party, preferably outdoors. Potatoes are not essential—although highly recommended—but a cooler full of cold beer, a good speaker, and a playlist of *norteño* (a popular music genre from northern Mexico) are.

Preheat a grill (griddle) over medium heat. Preheat the oven to 350°F/180°C/Gas Mark 4.

Put the potatoes in a large saucepan of cold water. Add 1 tablespoon of salt and bring to a boil over high heat. Cook for 15 minutes or until the potatoes are softened. Drain.

Cut a cross across the length of each potato, taking care not to slice all the way through. Open the potatoes slightly and add to each some butter, bacon, and parsley. Wrap the potatoes in aluminum foil and bake in the oven for 15 minutes.

Meanwhile, generously season the beef with salt and pepper. Place the meat on the grill and cook for 15 minutes, turning occasionally to prevent it from burning. Using a metal skewer, pierce the center, and if there is no resistance, transfer the meat to a cutting board. Set aside to rest for 2–3 minutes. Cut into 1-inch/2.5-cm-thick slices.

TO SERVE
Heat a skillet over high heat for 5 minutes. Add the tortillas, flipping them continuously for 2–3 minutes or until warmed through. Place the meat on a plate alongside the baked potatoes, lime wedges, and tortillas.

NORTHERN-STYLE BARBACOA TACOS

Prep time: 30 minutes, plus 2 hours marinating time
Cooking time: 1 hour
Makes: 4

For the barbacoa:
- 10 guajillo chiles, seeded and deveined
- 2 white onions, diced
- 6 cloves garlic
- 10 avocado leaves, toasted
- 10 black peppercorns
- 5 cloves
- ½ tablespoon ground cumin, toasted
- 1 tablespoon ground oregano, toasted
- ½ teaspoon salt
- 1 lb 2 oz/500 g beef sirloin
- 6 banana leaves

To serve:
- 4 Flour Tortillas (page 201)
- ½ white onion, finely chopped
- Chopped cilantro (coriander) leaves
- 4 lime wedges
- Your choice of sauces (pages 184–97)

This is a champion among steamed tacos. In northern Mexico, and across the river in the United States, they're morning tacos. However, the meat can be prepared the night before and stored, well wrapped, in the refrigerator. Reheat it using a steamer.

FOR THE BARBACOA
In a saucepan, combine the chiles, onions, garlic, avocado leaves, spices, and oregano. Add enough water to cover. Bring to a boil over high heat and boil for 7 minutes or until the chiles are softened. Drain.

Transfer the ingredients to a blender, add the salt, and blend into a smooth paste. Rub the beef with the adobo paste. Refrigerate for 2 hours to marinate.

In a steamer, place 12¾ cups (3 quarts/3 liters) of water in the bottom pan. Place 3 banana leaves at the bottom of the top pan, then put the marinated meat with the adobo paste and cover them with the remaining leaves. Steam over medium–high heat for 45 minutes. Check the bottom pan constantly, refilling it with water as needed to prevent burning. Remove and shred the meat.

TO SERVE
Heat a skillet over high heat for 5 minutes. Add the tortillas, flipping them continuously for 2–3 minutes or until warmed through.

Transfer to a plate, then top with the barbacoa meat. Serve with onion, cilantro (coriander), lime wedges, and any of our sauces on the side.

KOREAN TACOS

Prep time: 10 minutes, plus 30 minutes
marinating time
Cooking time: 5 minutes
Makes: 6–10

For the pork ribs:
- ⅔ cup (5 fl oz/150 ml) rice vinegar
- Scant ½ cup (3½ fl oz/100 ml) soy sauce
- Scant ½ cup (3½ fl oz/100 ml) mirin
- Scant ½ cup (3½ fl oz/100 ml) sake
- Scant ½ cup (3½ fl oz/100 ml) toasted sesame oil
- Scant ½ cup (3½ fl oz/100 ml) fish sauce
- ¼ cup (1¾ oz/50 g) sugar
- ¼ teaspoon salt
- ¼ teaspoon black pepper
- 1 lb 5 oz/600 g pork ribs, boneless and thinly sliced

To serve:
- 10 lettuce leaves
- 2 tablespoons kimchi (optional)

Korean cuisine and *chilango* (slang for something of or from Mexico City) cuisine embrace each other, extending around the world. The flavors, aromas, and forms are shared—what is a *saam* if not a form of taco, and what is a taco if not a form of *saam*? Only small details distinguish them from each other. Here, the kimchi is optional, but good kimchi is relatively easy to find, and we highly recommend using it.

FOR THE PORK RIBS
In a large bowl, combine all the ingredients except the ribs and mix well with a whisk.

Place the ribs on a cutting board and, using the back of the knife, gently pound the meat, so that it absorbs the marinade more easily. Add the ribs to the marinade, tossing to coat. Refrigerate for 30 minutes to marinate.

Heat a skillet over medium heat for 5 minutes. Add the ribs and 1 teaspoon of the marinade. Cook for 2–3 minutes or until the meat is cooked through and the marinade is dark and syrupy.

TO SERVE
Shape the lettuce leaves into cups, fill with the pork ribs, and top with kimchi, if using.

34   CLASSIC TACOS

YUCATÁN-STYLE COCHINITA PIBIL TACOS

Prep time: 20 minutes, plus 2 hours
marinating time
Cooking time: 1 hour 40 minutes
Makes: 4

For the cochinita pibil:
- 4 banana leaves
- 2 lb 4 oz/1 kg pork shoulder, bone-in
- 1 pineapple, grilled (3 lb 5 oz/1.5 kg)
- 1 large white onion, grilled
- 20 black peppercorns, toasted
- 10 cloves, toasted
- 3 cloves garlic, grilled
- 2 tablespoons salt
- 1 tablespoon ground oregano, toasted
- 1 teaspoon cumin seeds, toasted
- 1½ cups (9 oz/250 g) achiote chili paste
- 1¼ cups (10 fl oz/300 ml) white vinegar
- Juice of 10 sour oranges

To serve:
- 4 Corn Tortillas (page 200)
- Pickled Red Onions (page 190)
- Chopped Cilantro (coriander)
- 4 lime wedges

In the Yucatán, sour orange is an extremely common ingredient. If it's not readily available, it can be substituted with three parts regular orange juice and one part white vinegar.

FOR THE COCHINITA PIBIL
Line a baking dish with a banana leaf. Place the pork on top.

Put the remaining ingredients in a blender and blend into a smooth, thick paste. If necessary, add a little water. Pour the marinade over the pork, ensuring it's well coated. Cover with the remaining 3 banana leaves. Marinate in the refrigerator for 2 hours.

Preheat the oven to 400°F/200°C/ Gas Mark 6. Roast the pork for 1½ hours or until fork-tender. Remove from the oven, then shred the pork.

TO SERVE
Heat a skillet over high heat for 5 minutes. Add the tortillas, flipping them continuously for 2–3 minutes or until warmed through. Transfer to a plate, then top each with the cochinita pibil, pickled onion, and cilantro (coriander). Serve with lime wedges on the side.

BARBACOA TACOS

Prep time: 20 minutes
Cooking time: 2 hours 20 minutes
Makes: 4

For the barbacoa:
- 10 tomatoes, chopped
- 10 guajillo chiles, deveined and seeded
- 5 ancho chiles, deveined and seeded
- 5 dried chiles de árbol
- 2 white onions, diced
- 6 cloves garlic
- 10 black peppercorns
- 5 cloves
- 1 tablespoon ground oregano, toasted
- ½ tablespoon ground cumin
- 1 tablespoon salt
- 2 tablespoons olive oil
- 1 lb 5 oz/600 g brisket
- 10 banana leaves, toasted

To serve:
- 4 Corn Tortillas (page 200)
- ½ white onion, finely chopped
- Chopped cilantro (coriander) leaves
- Lime wedges
- Your choice of sauces (pages 184–97)

This is *barbacoa* as we speak of it in the pulque region of central Mexico. It is typically cooked in a pit and wrapped in maguey leaves, though here we suggest making it in the oven and wrapping it in banana leaves. Using brisket also makes it affordable.

FOR THE BARBACOA
In a large saucepan, combine all the ingredients except the salt, olive oil, beef, and banana leaves. Add enough water to cover. Bring to a boil over high heat and cook for 7 minutes, then reduce the heat to a simmer; cover and cook for a further 5 minutes or until the chiles are softened. Drain and transfer the mixture to a blender. Add the salt, then blend into a smooth paste. If necessary, add a little water to loosen.

Preheat the oven to 400°F/200°C/Gas Mark 6.

Heat the oil in a large saucepan over high heat. Add the beef and sear for 5 minutes on each side.

Line a baking dish with half of the banana leaves, then add the meat and the barbacoa paste. Add enough water to cover. Cover with the remaining banana leaves, then with aluminum foil. Roast for 2 hours or until fork-tender. Remove from the oven and shred the meat.

TO SERVE
Heat a skillet over high heat for 5 minutes. Add the tortillas, flipping them continuously for 2–3 minutes or until warmed through. Transfer to a plate, then top with the barbacoa meat. Serve with onion, cilantro (coriander), lime wedges, and any of our sauces on the side.

BAJA-STYLE FISH TACOS

TACOS DE PESCADO
ESTILO BAJA

Prep time: 20 minutes
Cooking time: 15 minutes
Makes: 4

For the battered fish:
- Vegetable oil, for deep-frying
- 2 cups (14 oz/400 g) all-purpose (plain) flour
- 1 teaspoon baking powder
- Pinch of salt
- Pinch of black pepper
- 4 skinless, boneless white fish fillets, cut into strips

For the cabbage salad:
- ¼ red cabbage, thinly sliced
- Thinly sliced red onion
- 1 tomato, diced
- 2 tablespoons Mayonnaise (page 184)
- Juice of 1 lime
- Pinch of salt

To serve:
- 4 Corn Tortillas (page 200)
- 4 lime wedges
- Your choice of sauces (pages 184–97)

This taco is a real classic from the cuisine of northwest Mexico. Our recipe here is the most accessible version for the home cook; in other recipes, light beer or sparkling water is added to the batter.

FOR THE BATTERED FISH
Heat a generous amount of oil in a deep skillet, about 1.5 inches/4 cm deep, over medium heat until it reaches 325°F–350°F/160°C–180°C.

In a bowl, combine the flour, baking powder, salt, and pepper. Gradually whisk in 1⅔ cups (14 fl oz/400 ml) of water. Coat the fish in the batter, gently removing any excess, then carefully lower into the hot oil. Fry for 4–5 minutes or until golden brown. Using tongs, transfer the fish to a paper towel–lined plate to absorb any excess oil.

FOR THE CABBAGE SALAD
Mix together all the ingredients in a bowl.

TO SERVE
Heat a skillet over high heat for 5 minutes. Add the tortillas, flipping them continuously for 2–3 minutes or until warmed through. Transfer to a plate, then top with the fish and cabbage salad. Serve with lime wedges and any of our sauces on the side.

SINALOA-STYLE FISH TACOS

Prep time: 20 minutes
Cooking time: 15 minutes
Makes: 4

For the battered fish:
- Vegetable oil, for deep-frying
- 2 cups (14 oz/400 g) all-purpose (plain) flour
- 1 teaspoon baking powder
- Pinch of salt
- Pinch of black pepper
- 1 egg
- 1⅔ cups (14 fl oz/400 ml) water or beer
- 4 white fish fillets, preferably mahi mahi

To serve:
- ¼ red cabbage, thinly sliced
- 2 tablespoons Mayonnaise (page 184)
- Juice of 1 lime
- Pinch of salt
- 4 Flour Tortillas (page 201)
- ¼ avocado, thinly sliced
- Pico de Gallo (page 191)
- 4 lime wedges
- Sinaloan Sauce (page 189)

Sinaloa is a state located in northwest Mexico. What makes this taco, more than its filling, are its accompaniments. Without the red cabbage, pico de gallo, and avocado, it just wouldn't be Sinaloan. The northern Mexico–style flour tortilla is also essential.

FOR THE BATTERED FISH
Heat a generous amount of oil in a deep skillet, about 1.5 inches/4 cm deep, over medium heat until it reaches 325°F–350°F/160°C–180°C.

In a bowl, combine the flour, baking powder, salt, and pepper. Whisk in the egg and the water or beer.

Coat the fish in the batter, gently removing any excess, then carefully lower into the hot oil. Fry for 4–5 minutes or until golden brown. Using tongs, transfer the fish to a paper towel–lined plate to absorb any excess oil.

TO SERVE
Mix together the cabbage, mayonnaise, lime juice, and salt in a large bowl.

Heat a skillet over high heat for 5 minutes. Add the tortillas, flipping them continuously for 2–3 minutes or until warmed through. Top the tortillas with the fish and serve with cabbage slaw, avocado, pico de gallo, lime wedges, and our Sinaloa-style sauces on the side.

CAPEADO TACOS

◗ ◆ ✿ *-30*

Prep time: 20 minutes
Cooking time: 7 minutes
Makes: 4

For the milanesa:
- Vegetable oil, for deep-frying
- 1 cup (7 oz/200 g) all-purpose (plain) flour
- 1 tablespoon black pepper
- 1 tablespoon dried oregano
- ½ tablespoon ground cumin
- ½ tablespoon salt
- ½ tablespoon garlic powder
- 2 eggs, beaten
- 2 cups (1 lb 2 oz/500 g) dry bread crumbs
- 2 lb 4 oz/1 kg thinly sliced beef tenderloin

To serve:
- 4 Corn Tortillas (page 200)
- ½ cup (4¼ oz/120 g) warmed refried beans
- Guacamole (page 190)
- 4 lime wedges, optional

The *milanesa* (breaded beef cutlet) taco is a constant presence in the stewed-tacos taco stand. You can accompany it, as in this recipe, with a smear of refried beans, but also—as with any other typical stewed taco—with a bit of red rice.

FOR THE MILANESA
Heat a generous amount of oil in a deep skillet, about 1 inch/2.5 cm deep, over high heat until it reaches 275°F/140°C.

In a shallow bowl, combine the flour, pepper, oregano, cumin, salt, and garlic powder. Put the eggs into a second bowl. Add the bread crumbs to a third bowl.

Coat the beef with the flour mixture, then with egg, and finally with bread crumbs. Gently lower the beef into the hot oil and fry for 5 minutes, until golden. Using a slotted spoon, transfer the beef to a paper towel–lined plate to drain any excess oil.

TO SERVE
Heat a skillet over high heat for 5 minutes. Add the tortillas, flipping them continuously for 2–3 minutes or until warmed through. Transfer each to a plate, then top with the beef milanesa and 1 tablespoon of refried beans. Serve with guacamole and lime wedges on the side.

VEGAN TACOS

Prep time: 30 minutes, plus 20 minutes resting time
Cooking time: 20 minutes
Makes: 4

For the vegan cutlets:
- Vegetable oil, for deep-frying, plus extra for moistening
- 3 cups (1 lb 2 oz/500 g) hard wheat (strong bread) flour, plus extra for dusting
- 20 g fresh yeast
- 1 tablespoon sugar
- 2 cups (1 lb 2 oz/500 g) dry bread crumbs
- 10 cloves, ground
- 1 tablespoon ground cumin
- 1 tablespoon ground oregano
- Pinch of salt

To serve:
- 4 Corn Tortillas (page 200)
- ½ white onion, finely chopped
- Chopped cilantro (coriander) leaves
- Lime wedges
- Your choice of salsas (pages 184–97)

These tacos could be seen as a canvas. If grated cooked potato was added to them, they would become *tortita de papa* tacos, or if sautéed scallions (spring onions) were added, they would have a Korean bent. Adding tomato broth makes them *tortitas de carne*, those classics of home cooking in Mexico City. Every taco is the promise of another taco.

FOR THE FILLING

Heat a generous amount of oil in a deep skillet, about 2 inches/5 cm deep, over high heat until it reaches 275°F/140°C.

In a stand mixer fitted with the whisk attachment, combine the flour, yeast, and sugar. Add 1 cup (8 fl oz/250 ml) of water and mix on medium speed for 20 minutes, until a dough forms. Cover the bowl with a damp cloth to prevent it from drying, then let rest for 20 minutes.

Transfer the rested dough to a lightly floured work surface. Divide the dough into 4 portions, roll into balls using your hands, then flatten them irregularly, like a beef cutlet.

In a shallow bowl, combine the bread crumbs, cloves, cumin, oregano, and salt. Using your hand, lightly moisten the cutlets with a little oil, then coat them in bread crumbs, ensuring they are entirely covered.

Gently lower the cutlets into the hot oil and fry for 5 minutes, turning once, until golden. Using tongs, transfer the cutlets to a paper towel–lined plate to drain any excess oil. Slice the cutlets.

TO SERVE

Heat a skillet over high heat for 5 minutes. Add the tortillas, flipping them continuously for 2–3 minutes or until warmed through. Place a cutlet on each tortilla. Serve with onion, cilantro (coriander), lime wedges, and any of our salsas on the side.

CRUNCHY AL PASTOR TACOS

Prep time: 20 minutes
Cooking time: 7 minutes
Makes: 4

- Vegetable oil, for frying
- 10½ oz/300 g Pastor meat (page 104 [Tacos al Pastor])
- 4 Corn Tortillas (page 200)
- 3 roasted sliced prickly pears
- ½ white onion, thinly sliced
- 2 tomatoes, finely chopped
- 5 sprigs cilantro (coriander), chopped
- Juice of 1 lime
- Pinch of salt

To serve:
- 4 lime wedges
- Your choice of sauces (pages 184–97)

This is a not-so-common variety of *al pastor* taco but it is equally delicious—perhaps even more so, thanks to its crunchy texture. Outside the home, it appears in those mountains of tacos found at some select taquerías in downtown Mexico City.

Heat a generous amount of oil in a skillet over low heat.

Heat another skillet over high heat for 5 minutes. Add the tortillas, flipping them continuously for 2–3 minutes or until warmed through.

Fill each tortilla with the pastor meat, then roll them up into little "cigars."

In a bowl, combine the roasted prickly pear, onion, tomatoes, cilantro (coriander), and lime juice. Season to taste.

Carefully lower the filled tacos into the hot oil and fry for 5 minutes, until golden. Using tongs, transfer the tacos to a paper towel–lined plate to remove any excess oil.

TO SERVE
Arrange the tacos on a long platter, then spoon the prickly pear salad over the top. Serve with lime wedges and any of our sauces on the side.

TRIPE TACOS

Prep time: 20 minutes
Cooking time: 1 hour
Makes: 4

For the beef tripe:
- 1 lb 2 oz/500 g beef tripe, cleaned
- 2¼ cups (17 fl oz/500 ml) whole (full-fat) milk
- ¼ white onion, chopped
- 3 cloves garlic
- 5 dried bay leaves
- 3 sprigs dried thyme
- 3 sprigs dried marjoram
- ¾ teaspoon salt
- 1 lb 2 oz/500 g lard or oil

To serve:
- 4 Corn Tortillas (page 200)
- 1 lb 2 oz/500 g Beef Tripe
- ½ white onion, diced
- 6 sprigs cilantro (coriander), coarsely chopped
- 4 lime wedges
- Your choice of sauces (pages 184–97)

The tripe in this recipe is cooked twice—some taquerías even cook it thrice. We recommend browning it on the grill for added texture.

FOR THE BEEF TRIPE
In a large saucepan, combine all the ingredients except the lard. Stir in 4½ cups (34 fl oz/1 liter) of water. Simmer for 30 minutes on medium–high heat or until the meat is very tender. Drain.

Heat a skillet over medium heat. Add the lard or oil to the pan, then add the tripe and add water until the meat is covered. Cook for 10 minutes.

Increase the heat to high and sauté for 5 minutes, stirring continuously to prevent it from burning. Cook uncovered for a further 10 minutes or until the tripe is golden. Drain. Transfer the tripe to a cutting board and coarsely chop.

TO SERVE
Heat a skillet over high heat for 5 minutes. Add the tortillas, flipping them continuously for 2–3 minutes or until warmed through. Transfer to a plate, top with the meat, onion, and cilantro (coriander). Serve with lime wedges and any of our sauces on the side.

MICHOACÁN-STYLE CARNITAS TACOS

Prep time: 20 minutes
Cooking time: 1 hour
Makes: 4

For the carnitas:
- 1 lb 2 oz/500 g lard
- 2 lb 4 oz/1 kg pork leg or rib
- Juice of 1 lb 2 oz/500 g sour orange, peels reserved
- ½ cup (3½ oz/100 g) sugar
- 4 cloves garlic
- 2 white onions, diced
- 20 dried bay leaves
- 10 cloves
- 10 sprigs thyme
- 10 sprigs marjoram
- 1 tablespoon black pepper
- ¼ teaspoon salt

To serve:
- 4 Corn Tortillas (page 200)
- Chopped cilantro (coriander) leaves
- ½ white onion, finely chopped
- Lime wedges
- Your choice of sauces (pages 184–97)

The copper pan traditionally used in this recipe is typical in the state of Michoacán, where there are many copper mines. Sure, you could use any pan. But truly, get yourself a copper one: it won't be particularly expensive, it's useful for all kinds of stews and confits, and it will probably last you a lifetime—and several generations thereafter. It will also help distribute the cooking heat evenly.

FOR THE CARNITAS
Heat the lard in a large, preferably copper, saucepan over medium heat. Add all the remaining ingredients and bring to a boil. Reduce the heat to medium–low, and simmer for 1 hour or until the meat is tender throughout. Stir occasionally with a wooden spoon, to prevent burning.

Using a slotted spoon, transfer the pork to a cutting board. Remove the meat from the bone and cut into uniform pieces.

TO SERVE
Heat a skillet over high heat for 5 minutes. Add the tortillas, flipping them continuously for 2–3 minutes or until warmed through. Transfer to a plate and top each tortilla with carnitas. Serve with cilantro (coriander), onion, lime wedges, and any of our sauces on the side.

CARNITAS CHILANGAS TACOS

TACOS DE CARNITAS CHILANGAS

Prep time: 20 minutes
Cooking time: 1 hour
Makes: 4

For the carnitas:
- 2 lb 4 oz/1 kg pork lard
- 1 lb 2 oz/500 g pork leg or rib
- 20 dried bay leaves
- 1 tablespoon black pepper
- 10 cloves
- 10 sprigs thyme
- 10 sprigs marjoram
- 2 white onions, diced
- 4 cloves garlic
- ¼ teaspoon salt

To serve:
- 4 Corn Tortillas (page 200)
- 10 sprigs cilantro (coriander), chopped
- ½ white onion, finely chopped
- Lime wedges
- Your choice of sauces (pages 184–97)

The preparation of carnitas in Mexico City has undergone an "urbanization" process, which involved using some different ingredients from the original recipe: Fanta instead of orange juice, for example. At Cosme, we use Carnation milk and Coca-Cola to prepare them, as it was done at Pujol a few years ago.

FOR THE CARNITAS
Heat the lard in a large, preferably copper, saucepan over medium heat. Add the remaining ingredients and bring to a boil. Reduce the heat to medium–low, and simmer, stirring occasionally with a wooden spoon to prevent burning, for 1 hour or until the meat is tender throughout.

Using a slotted spoon, transfer the pork to a cutting board. Remove the meat from the bone and cut into uniform pieces.

TO SERVE
Heat a skillet over high heat for 5 minutes. Add the tortillas, flipping them continuously for 2–3 minutes or until warmed through. Transfer to a plate and top each tortilla with carnitas. Serve with cilantro (coriander), onion, lime wedges, and any of our sauces on the side.

MONTERREY-STYLE CHICHARRÓN TACOS

TACOS DE CHICHARRÓN ESTILO MONTERREY

Prep time: 20 minutes, plus 1 hour marinating time
Cooking time: 30 minutes
Makes: 4

For the chicharrones:
- 4½ cups (34 fl oz/1 liter) whole (full-fat) milk
- 1½ teaspoons garlic powder
- 1½ teaspoons onion powder
- ¼ teaspoon ground cumin
- ¼ teaspoon black pepper
- ¾ teaspoon salt
- ¼ cup (4 fl oz/120 ml) white vinegar
- 1 lb 2 oz/500 g pork jowl, cleaned and cut into strips
- 1 lb 2 oz/500 g pork lard

To serve:
- 4 Corn Tortillas (page 200)
- Pico de Gallo (page 191)
- Guacamole (page 190)
- Lime wedges

Surprisingly easy to make, the chicharrones (pork rinds) here are a variation of the chicharrones typically available on weekends at butcher shops, whether in Monterrey or elsewhere in Mexico. In some butcher shops, they're packed in takeout bags. The portability is essential, and so is a little lime to go with them.

FOR THE CHICHARRONES
Put all the ingredients except the lard and meat in a blender and blend well. Transfer the marinade to a large bowl and add the meat, tossing to coat with the marinade. Marinate in the refrigerator for 1 hour.

Preheat the oven to 400°F/200°C/Gas Mark 6.

Drain the meat, then transfer it to a roasting dish. Cover with aluminum foil and roast for 20 minutes.

Heat the lard in a saucepan over medium heat, until it reaches 275°F/140°C. Carefully add the pork jowl and stir constantly for 7 minutes or until it is golden and crispy. Using a slotted spoon, transfer the chicharrones to a paper towel–lined plate to drain any excess oil, then cut into large cubes.

TO SERVE
Heat a skillet over high heat for 5 minutes. Add the tortillas, flipping them continuously for 2–3 minutes or until warmed through. Place the chicharrones on a plate, then add the pico de gallo and guacamole. Serve with tortillas and lime wedges on the side.

SUADERO TACOS

Prep time: 20 minutes
Cooking time: 45 minutes
Makes: 8

For the suadero:
- 1 lb 2 oz/500 g brisket
- 1 white onion, diced
- 3 cloves garlic
- 10 dried bay leaves
- 5 sprigs dried thyme
- 1 tablespoon salt
- Generous 2 cups (17 fl oz/500 ml) vegetable oil

To serve:
- 8 Corn Tortillas (page 200)
- ½ white onion, finely chopped
- Cilantro (coriander), chopped
- Lime wedges
- Your choice of salsas (pages 184–97)

There is a variety of suadero tacos; this one is characterized by the meat being fried in its own fat (like with carnitas). Suadero tacos are defined not so much by the recipe as by the cut of meat used. We want to ensure that these tacos are served in the traditional way, with great care taken at every step, from the quality of meat used to the cooking time and even the cooking temperature. Only once the traditional cooking process has been ensured do we get creative, accompanying them with ingredients other than the classic onion and cilantro (coriander), or pairing it with a certain sauce.

But for this quintessential taco of Mexico City, the raw onion and cilantro *are* essential, and the lime juice is squeezed over it just before the bite—this is what makes it chilango. The cooked green sauce Green Serrano Salsa (page 194) is canonical.

FOR THE SUADERO
Put the meat, onion, garlic, and herbs in a pressure cooker. Add enough water to cover. Cook on high for 30 minutes. Drain the meat, discarding the cooking liquid.

Place a large saucepan over medium–high heat. Add the oil and a generous 2 cups (17 fl oz/500 ml) of water. Bring to a boil, add the meat, and cook for 10–15 minutes on medium–low heat. Transfer the suadero to a cutting board and chop into bite-size pieces.

TO SERVE
Heat a skillet over high heat for 5 minutes. Add the tortillas, flipping them continuously for 2–3 minutes or until warmed through. Transfer to a plate and top each tortilla with suadero. Serve with onion, cilantro (coriander), lime wedges, and any of our salsas on the side.

SWEET PORK BELLY TACOS

Prep time: 20 minutes
Cooking time: 30 minutes
Makes: 4

- 1 lb 2 oz/500 g pork belly
- 1 tablespoon salt
- 8½ cups (68 fl oz/2 liters) vegetable oil

To serve:
- 4 tablespoons sweet plum sauce
- 4 Flour Tortillas (page 201)
- 1 cucumber, thinly sliced
- Chopped scallions (spring onions)
- 4 lime wedges
- Your choice of salsas (pages 184–97)

This taco is a variation of the Yucatecan *castacan*: pieces of the pork belly with some of the skin attached. It is served with a simple salad, an important part of the taco. The vegetables provide an element of freshness.

Place the pork belly and salt in a pressure cooker. Add enough water to cover, then cook on medium heat for 20 minutes. Drain.

Heat the oil in a saucepan over low heat until it reaches 275°F/140°C. Add the pork belly and cook for 5 minutes or until golden. Using a slotted spoon, transfer the meat to a paper towel–lined plate to drain any excess oil. Once cool enough to handle, cut into thin slices.

TO SERVE
In a bowl, coat the pork belly with the sweet plum sauce.

Heat a skillet over high heat for 5 minutes. Add the tortillas, flipping them continuously for 2–3 minutes or until warmed through. Transfer to a plate and top each tortilla with pork belly. Serve with cucumber, scallion (spring onion), lime wedges, and any of our salsas on the side.

DUCK TACOS

Prep time: 20 minutes, plus 5 hours drying time
Cooking time: 1 hour 30 minutes
Makes: 10

- 1 duck, cleaned
- 3 star anise
- 1 tablespoon ground cinnamon
- 1 tablespoon black pepper
- 1 tablespoon finely chopped ginger
- ¼ teaspoon salt
- 2 cloves garlic, finely chopped
- 6 tablespoons honey
- 2 tablespoons rice vinegar
- 1 tablespoon soy sauce

To serve:
- 10 Flour Tortillas (page 201)
- Your choice of salsas (pages 184–97)

For this taco, inspired by Chinatown neighborhood cuisine, the tortillas can be replaced with rice papers. You can also serve these tacos with a little hoisin sauce, if you like.

Let the cleaned duck dry in a ventilated room for at least 5 hours or until the skin is very dry to the touch.

In a skillet over medium heat, combine all the remaining ingredients, along with 2 tablespoons of water. Using a rubber spatula, stir frequently for 5–7 minutes or until syrupy.

Preheat the oven to 400°F/200°C/Gas Mark 6. Place the duck in a baking dish, then pour in the hot mixture. Roast uncovered for 15 minutes.

Reduce the temperature to 300°F/150°C/Gas Mark 4. Cook the duck for another 1 hour, pouring over the cooking liquid every 10 minutes to baste. Using a metal skewer, pierce the duck through the center. If there is any resistance, cook for another 5 minutes.

TO SERVE
Heat a skillet over high heat for 5 minutes. Add the tortillas, flipping them continuously for 2–3 minutes or until warmed through. Place the whole duck without its cooking juices on a platter, and serve it with tortillas and any of our salsas on the side.

PORK WITH ORANGE TACOS

Prep time: 20 minutes
Cooking time: 1 hour
Makes: 8

For the carnitas:
- 10½ oz/300 g pork lard
- Scant 1 cup (7 fl oz/200 ml) vegetable oil
- Juice of 1 lb 2 oz/500 g oranges, peels reserved
- ½ cup (3½ oz/100 g) sugar
- ½ white onion, diced
- 4 cloves garlic
- 10 dried bay leaves
- 10 cloves
- 10 sprigs thyme
- 10 sprigs marjoram
- 1 teaspoon salt
- ½ tablespoon black pepper
- 10½ oz/300 g pork leg or rib

To serve:
- 8 Corn Tortillas (page 200)
- Chopped cilantro (coriander) leaves
- ¼ white onion, finely chopped
- Lime wedges
- Your choice of sauces (pages 184–97)

For this recipe you will want to use a copper saucepan, as it will distribute the heat evenly. However, if you don't have one, you can use a regular metal saucepan—just be sure to keep an eye on the meat during cooking time. In taquerías, the cooked meat is often kept warm under an incandescent light bulb until ready to use, which is how the recipe gets its name.

FOR THE CARNITAS
Heat the pork lard and oil in a copper saucepan over medium heat, then add all the ingredients, including the orange peels. Simmer for 1 hour or until the meat is tender throughout, stirring frequently with a wooden spoon to prevent it from burning.

Transfer the pork to a strainer to drain off any excess fat. Transfer to a cutting board, remove the meat from the bone and cut into bite-sized pieces.

TO SERVE
Heat a skillet over high heat for 5 minutes. Add the tortillas, flipping them continuously for 2–3 minutes or until warmed through. Transfer to a plate, then top with the carnitas. Serve with cilantro (coriander), onion, lime wedges, and any of our sauces on the side.

HARD-SHELL TACOS

Prep time: 30 minutes
Cooking time: 20 minutes
Makes: 4

For the filling:
- 2 tablespoons olive oil
- ½ white onion, finely chopped
- 3 cloves garlic, finely chopped
- 7 oz/200 g bacon, finely chopped
- 10½ oz/300 g ground (minced) beef
- 10½ oz/300 g ground (minced) pork
- 2 tablespoons soy sauce
- 1 tablespoon Dijon mustard
- 1 tablespoon Worcestershire sauce
- ½ teaspoon black pepper
- Salt

To serve:
- 4 crispy corn tortillas (store-bought)
- Guacamole (page 190)
- Pico de Gallo (page 191)
- 2 lettuce leaves, chopped
- Lime wedges

In the late 1990s, due to the mass commercialization of taco fast food spots, the hard-shell taco became increasingly popular. Our years, maturity, and openness have made us see the representative hard-shell taco in a better light.

FOR THE FILLING
Heat the oil in a large skillet over high heat. Add the onion, garlic, and bacon and sauté for 5 minutes or until the mixture begins to brown. Add the beef and pork and sauté for 10 minutes, until the meat is cooked through. Stir in the soy sauce, mustard, and Worcestershire sauce, Season with the pepper and salt.

TO SERVE
Fill the tortillas with the meat filling. Top with guacamole, pico de gallo, and lettuce. Serve with lime wedges on the side.

BEEF FLAUTAS

Prep time: 20 minutes
Cooking time: 45 minutes
Makes: 4

For the flautas:
- 10½ oz/300 g beef brisket
- 5 dried bay leaves
- 1 tablespoon salt, plus extra to season
- 2 tablespoons olive oil
- 1 white onion, finely chopped
- 2 cloves garlic, finely chopped
- 3 tomatoes, finely chopped
- 4½ cups (34 fl oz/1 liter) vegetable oil
- 8 large Corn Tortillas (page 200)

To serve:
- ½ head iceberg lettuce, thinly sliced
- ½ white onion, thinly sliced
- 4 tablespoons crumbled panela cheese
- 4 tablespoons sour cream
- Lime wedges

Few things are as beautiful as the Michoacán-style diners that appeared in Mexico City in the 1950s. They are distinguished by the green color of their walls, the small wooden benches for seating, and elongated display cases containing rows and rows of *flautas*, or "flutes," both cooked and waiting to be cooked. These beef *flautas* (they could also be pork or chicken) are an homage to those diners, which are fading away, soon to be only a memory.

FOR THE FLAUTAS

Place the brisket, bay leaves, and salt in a large saucepan. Add enough water to cover. Bring to a boil over high heat, then reduce the heat to medium–low, and simmer for 25 minutes. Drain, then shred the meat.

Heat the olive oil in a skillet over medium–high heat. Add the onion and garlic, and sauté for 10 minutes or until the onion is golden. Add the tomatoes and sauté for another 10 minutes or until the tomatoes are cooked through and most of their juices have evaporated. Stir in the brisket and season with salt. Set aside.

Heat the vegetable oil in a deep fryer or deep saucepan over high heat until it reaches 350°F/180°C. Spoon the brisket mixture down the center of the tortillas, then roll them tightly into "flutes." Secure the ends with toothpicks (cocktail sticks) to prevent the flautas from unraveling. Carefully lower into the hot oil and deep-fry for 5 minutes or until golden and crispy. Using a slotted spoon, transfer to a paper towel–lined plate to drain any excess oil.

TO SERVE

Arrange the flautas on a platter and remove the picks. Top with the lettuce, onion, cheese, and cream. Serve with lime wedges on the side.

BRISKET FLAUTAS

Prep time: 20 minutes
Cooking time: 2 hours
Makes: 8

For the flautas:
- 10½ oz/300 g beef brisket
- 5 dried bay leaves
- ¼ teaspoon salt, plus extra to season
- 2 tablespoons olive oil
- 1 white onion, finely chopped
- 2 cloves garlic, finely chopped
- 3 tomatoes, finely chopped
- 4½ cups (34 fl oz/1 liter) vegetable oil
- 8 large Corn Tortillas (page 200)

To serve:
- Manzano Chile Tomato Sauce (page 197)
- ½ head iceberg lettuce, thinly sliced
- 4 tablespoons panela cheese
- 4 tablespoons sour cream
- ½ white onion, thinly sliced
- Lime wedges

In Mexico, there is a widespread custom of drenching food in sauce. There is something very pleasing about having the sauce soak the dishes. In this case, the crunchiness of the *flautas* combined with the abundance of sauce results in a winning combination.

FOR THE FLAUTAS

Place the brisket, bay leaves, and salt in a large saucepan. Add enough water to cover. Bring to a boil over high heat, then reduce the heat to medium–low, and simmer for 90 minutes. Drain, then shred the meat.

Heat the olive oil in a skillet over medium–high heat. Add the onion and garlic, and sauté for 10 minutes or until the onion is golden. Add the tomatoes and sauté for another 10 minutes or until the tomatoes are cooked through and most of their juice has evaporated. Stir in the brisket and season with salt. Set aside.

Heat the vegetable oil in a deep fryer or deep saucepan over high heat until it reaches 356°F/180°C. Spoon the brisket mixture down the center of the tortillas, then roll them tightly into "flutes." Secure the ends with toothpicks (cocktail sticks) to prevent the flautas from unraveling. Carefully lower into the hot oil and deep-fry for 3 minutes or until golden and crispy. Using a slotted spoon, transfer to a paper towel–lined plate to drain any excess oil.

TO SERVE

Arrange the flautas on a platter and remove the picks. Slather with chile sauce, then top with lettuce, cheese, cream, and onion. Serve with lime wedges on the side.

PORK BELLY AND CRACKLING TACOS

Prep time: 20 minutes
Cooking time: 40 minutes
Makes: 4

- ¼ teaspoon salt
- 1 lb 2 oz/500 g pork belly
- 10½ oz/300 g pork lard
- 2 cups (17 fl oz/500 ml) vegetable oil, plus extra for greasing
- Charred Green Salsa (page 193)
- 4 Corn Tortillas (page 200), to serve
- Your choice of spicy salsas (pages 184–97), to serve

This dish is chicharrones (pork rinds) in green sauce—but taken to the next level. It can be seen as a stewed taco, though common in Mexican Northern states, it's not a common option in the stews of Mexico City. It would be very good with red rice or refried beans on the side.

Fill a saucepan with water, add the salt, and place over medium–high heat. Add the pork belly and cook for 20 minutes. Using a spider or slotted spoon, transfer the pork belly to a paper towel–lined plate or baking sheet to drain any excess.

Heat the lard and oil in a saucepan on high heat. Fry the pork belly for 5 minutes or until golden. Drain, then roughly chop into chichar-rones. Reserve.

Grease a saucepan with vegetable oil. Add the green salsa and simmer over medium heat for 10 minutes. Then place the chicharrones in the salsa 5 minutes before serving to prevent them from getting soggy.

Meanwhile, to serve, heat a skillet over high heat for 5 minutes. Add the tortillas, flipping them con-tinuously for 2–3 minutes or until warmed through.

Transfer the chicharrones to a deep plate, which will help them absorb the sauce without losing their char-acteristic crispy texture. Serve with the warmed tortillas and any of our spicy salsas on the side.

BATTERED STEW TACOS

TACOS DE GUISADO CAPEADOS

Prep time: 20 minutes
Cooking time: 30 minutes
Makes: 4

For the rice:
- ½ cup (3½ oz/100 g) rice
- 2 tablespoons olive oil
- 1 large tomato
- ½ clove garlic
- ¼ white onion, chopped
- ¼ teaspoon salt

For the chiles:
- 4 poblano chiles
- 4½ cups (34 fl oz/1 liter) vegetable oil
- 3 eggs

- 1 cup (7 oz/200 g) all-purpose (plain) flour
- 14 oz/400 g panela cheese, sliced into 4 equal pieces
- 2 cups (8½ oz/240 g) chicharrones (page 72)

To serve:
- 4 Corn Tortillas (page 200)
- Red Morita Salsa (page 194)

These battered chile relleno tacos call for pork chicharrones, which are then bathed in morita chile sauce. They are easily converted to vegetarian tacos by doubling the cheese and eliminating the chicharrones. Another option is to substitute the fresh poblano chile for its dried (rehydrated) version, the ancho chile. That's how they make them at La Hortaliza tacos in the Condesa neighborhood in Mexico City, and they're fantastic.

FOR THE RICE
Place the rice in a bowl, then cover it with water. Using your hand, slowly move the grains around, taking care not to break them. Drain and repeat the process until the water runs clear.

Heat 2 tablespoons of the olive oil in a large saucepan over medium–high heat until the oil is hot. Add the washed rice and, using a wooden spoon to stir constantly, sauté for a few minutes until the rice has browned.

In a blender, combine the tomato, garlic, onion, and salt. Add scant 1 cup (7 fl oz/210 ml) of water and blend. Pour the mixture into the saucepan. Cook until one-quarter of the liquid remains, then cover and reduce the heat to low. Cook for another 10 minutes.

FOR THE CHILES
Roast the chiles over direct heat until charred and blistered. Transfer them to a lidded container or a bowl and cover with the lid or plastic wrap (clingfilm), to sweat them and make the skin and seeds easier to remove.

Heat the vegetable oil in a deep fryer or deep saucepan over high heat until it reaches 275°F/140°C.

Beat the eggs in a deep bowl until fluffy. Place the flour in a bowl.

Remove the skin from the cooled chiles, then cut them open at the stem end, discarding the tops, and remove the seeds. Fill the chiles with a piece of panela and scant ½ cup chicharrones. Coat the chiles in the flour, then dip them in the egg. Gently lower the stuffed chiles into the hot oil and deep-fry for 4–5 minutes or until the coating is golden.

TO SERVE
Heat a skillet over high heat for 5 minutes. Add the tortillas, flipping them continuously for 2–3 minutes or until warmed through. Place a spoonful of rice and a stuffed chile on each tortilla. Serve with red morita sauce.

STEW TACOS

Prep time: 20 minutes
Cooking time: 1 hour 15 minutes
Makes: 8

For the bean paste:
- Scant ½ cup (3½ oz/100 g) black beans, soaked overnight
- ¼ teaspoon salt
- 2 tablespoons olive oil
- 1 white onion, finely chopped
- 2 cloves garlic, finely chopped
- 2 dried chiles de árbol

For the stew:
- 2 tablespoons olive oil
- 10½ oz/300 g Red Serrano Salsa (page 195)
- 10½ oz/300 g pork chicharrones (see page 56)

To serve:
- 8 Corn Tortillas (page 200)
- Your choice of sauces (pages 184–97)

This is a stew taco—with pork chicharrones in red sauce—though the method is applicable to any other taco too. This bean paste can be used for other tacos or many other things.

FOR THE BEAN PASTE
Place the beans in a saucepan, then add twice the amount of water. Add the salt. Bring to a boil, then cover and reduce the heat to medium–low. Simmer for 45 minutes or until the beans are softened.

Heat the oil in a saucepan over medium heat. Add the onion and garlic, and sauté for 15 minutes or until the onion is caramelized. Add the beans with their cooking liquid and the chiles and cook for 15 minutes. Transfer the mixture to a blender and blend into a homogeneous paste.

FOR THE STEW
Heat the oil in a saucepan over medium heat. Add the red serrano salsa and cook for 10 minutes. Stir in the chicharrones and cook for 2–3 minutes.

TO SERVE
Heat a skillet over high heat for 5 minutes. Add the tortillas, flipping them continuously for 2–3 minutes or until warmed through. Transfer to a plate and top each tortilla with 1 tablespoon of bean paste and 1 tablespoon of stew. Serve with any of our sauces on the side.

STEWED TACOS

Prep time: 20 minutes
Cooking time: 30 minutes
Makes: 4

For the ribs:
- 2 lb 4 oz/500 g pork rib with bone, cut into cubes
- ½ tablespoon salt
- scant 1 cup (7 fl oz/210 ml) water

For the rice and sauce:
- ½ cup (3½ oz/100 g) rice
- 4 tablespoons olive oil
- 1 large tomatoes
- 1 cloves garlic
- ¼ white onions
- ½ teaspoon salt

- 3½ lb oz/100 g Green Tomato-Pasilla Salsa (see page 195)

To serve:
- 4 Corn Tortillas (page 200)

This taco uses a specific stew—pork in pasilla chile sauce—although any stew can go into a taco. Use the mold of this taco for whatever is left over from yesterday: shredded chicken in green mole, chayote in *pipián*, steak in a morita chile sauce or "a la mexicana" (serrano chile, onion, and tomato).

Place the rice in a bowl, then cover it with water. Using your hand, slowly move the grains around, taking care not to break them. Drain and repeat the process until the water runs clear.

FOR THE RIBS
Set the pressure cooker to high and add the ribs, salt, and water until the ingredients are covered. Let it pressure cook for 20 minutes.

FOR THE SAUCE
In a saucepan, heat 2 tablespoons of oil over medium–high heat. When the oil is hot, add the washed rice and, using a wooden spoon to stir constantly, sauté until the rice has browned.

In a blender, combine the tomatoes, garlic, onion, and salt. Add the remaining water and blend. Pour the mixture into the saucepan. Cook until one-quarter of the liquid remains, then cover and reduce the heat to low. Cook for another 10 minutes.

Place a saucepan over high heat, grease it with 2 tablespoons of oil, then add the Green Tomato-Pasilla Salsa and meat along with all the cooking liquid. Cook for 10 minutes, stirring, to meld the flavors.

TO SERVE
Heat a skillet over high heat for 5 minutes. Add the tortillas, flipping them continuously for 2–3 minutes or until warmed through. Transfer to a plate and top each tortilla with 1 tablespoon of red rice, and 1 tablespoon of stew.

PICKLED TURKEY TACOS

TACOS DE PAVO
EN ESCABECHE

Prep time: 10 minutes, plus 30 minutes
marinating time
Cooking time: 40 minutes
Makes: 4

For the pickled turkey:
- 10 sprigs thyme, ground
- 10 dried bay leaves
- ¼ teaspoon ground cinnamon
- ½ teaspoon ground oregano
- ½ teaspoon ground cumin
- ½ teaspoon black pepper
- ¼ teaspoon ground cloves
- ½ teaspoon salt, divided
- 1 tablespoon olive oil
- 1 large white onion, coarsely chopped

- 3 cloves garlic, chopped
- Generous 2 cups (17 fl oz/500 ml) white vinegar
- ½ skinless, boneless turkey breast (1 lb 2 oz/500 g)

To serve:
- 4 Corn Tortillas (page 200)
- Pickled chiles
- Your choice of sauces (pages 184–97)

The wild turkey or *kutz* (in Maya) is the prince of the birds in Yucatán, from where this recipe originates. It's elegant, ceremonious, and nonchalant. It has blue-green iridescent spots on its beautiful wings.

If you're not in a rush, the escabeche will benefit from resting a night in the refrigerator.

FOR THE PICKLED TURKEY
Combine all the spices and ¼ teaspoon of the salt in a small bowl. Generously rub the seasoning over the turkey, ensuring it's well coated. Refrigerate for 30 minutes to marinate.

Heat the oil in a saucepan over high heat. Add the onion and garlic, reduce the heat to medium, and sauté for 10 minutes or until the onion is golden. Add the vinegar, turkey, and remaining ¼ teaspoon of salt. Add enough water to cover the turkey. Cook for 20 minutes or until the meat is very tender. Remove from the heat and shred the meat.

TO SERVE
Heat a skillet over high heat for 5 minutes. Add the tortillas, flipping them continuously for 2–3 minutes or until warmed through. Transfer to a plate and top each tortilla with shredded turkey. Serve with pickled chiles and any of our sauces on the side.

TIJUANA-STYLE BIRRIA TACOS

Prep time: 20 minutes
Cooking time: 50 minutes
Makes: 4

For the beef birria:
- 9 oz/250 g beef ribs
- 9 oz/250 g beef shank
- 2 tablespoons salt

For the sauce:
- 2 tablespoons olive oil
- 10 guajillo chiles, seeded and deveined
- 5 pasilla chiles, seeded and deveined
- 2 morita chiles, seeded and deveined
- 10 dried bay leaves
- 5 cloves, toasted
- 6 tomatoes, chopped
- 1 large white onion

- 4 cloves garlic
- ½ tablespoon black pepper, toasted
- ¼ teaspoon salt

To serve:
- 4 Corn Tortillas (page 200)
- 4 tablespoons cooked bayo beans (or any other bean)
- Chopped cilantro (coriander) leaves
- 1 serrano chile, chopped with seeds
- ½ white onion, finely chopped
- Lime wedges
- Your choice of sauces (pages 184–97)

The main difference between Tijuana-style birria and Jalisco-style birria (see page 84) is the protein: beef dominates in Tijuana, while goat is king in Jalisco.

FOR THE BEEF BIRRIA
Place the beef ribs and shank and the salt in a pressure cooker. Add enough water to cover the meat. Cook on medium–high for 20 minutes, until the valve starts releasing hot steam. Drain, reserving the cooking broth. Shred the meat.

FOR THE SAUCE
Heat the olive oil in a deep saucepan over medium heat. Add the remaining ingredients and stir constantly for 7 minutes to prevent burning. Stir in the shredded beef and reserved cooking broth. Boil for 20 minutes.

TO SERVE
Heat a skillet over high heat for 5 minutes. Add the tortillas, flipping them continuously for 2–3 minutes or until warmed through. Transfer to a plate and top each tortilla with 2–3 tablespoons of birria, 1 table-spoon of bayo beans, the cilantro (coriander), chile, and onion. Serve with lime wedges and any of our sauces on the side.

JALISCO-STYLE BIRRIA TACOS

Prep time: 20 minutes, plus 1 hour
marinating time
Cooking time: 1 hour 30 minutes
Makes: 8

For the goat birria:
- 4 tomatoes
- 3 cloves garlic
- ½ large white onion
- 8 guajillo chiles, seeded and deveined
- 5 ancho chiles, seeded and deveined
- 5 cascabel chiles, seeded and deveined
- 2 morita chiles
- 10 dried bay leaves
- 5 cloves, toasted
- ¼ teaspoon black pepper, toasted
- ¼ teaspoon salt
- 7 oz/500 g goat meat
- 2 tablespoons olive oil

To serve:
- 8 Corn Tortillas (page 200)
- 4 tablespoons cooked bayo beans
- Finely chopped white onion
- 1 serrano chile, chopped with seeds
- Chopped cilantro (coriander) leaves
- 4 lime wedges
- Your choice of sauces (pages 184–97), to serve

In birria tacos, it is common to use "mixtas" tortillas, which are made with nixtamalized corn and wheat flour, giving them the elasticity of flour tortillas with the flavor of corn tortillas. These tortillas are often found on the road, in Vallarta, where birria is sold.

FOR THE GOAT BIRRIA
Half-fill a saucepan with water and bring to a boil over high heat. Add all the ingredients except the meat and olive oil and cook for 15 minutes or until the chiles are softened.

Transfer the mixture to a blender and puree. In a large bowl, coat the meat with the mixture. Refrigerate for 1 hour to marinate.

Heat the oil in a saucepan over high heat for 5 minutes. Add the meat with its marinade and cook, stirring, for 5 minutes. Add enough water to cover. Bring to a boil, reduce the heat, and boil for 1 hour over medium heat.

TO SERVE
Heat a skillet over high heat for 5 minutes. Add the tortillas, flipping them continuously for 2–3 minutes or until warmed through. Transfer to a plate and top each tortilla with 2–3 tablespoons of birria, 1 table-spoon of bayo beans, onion, serrano chile, and cilantro (coriander). Serve with lime wedges and any of our sauces on the side.

CHAMORRO TACOS

Prep time: 15 minutes
Cooking time: 3 hours
Makes: 6

- 7 cloves garlic
- 7 oz/200 g achiote bars
- 2 large white onions
- 1 tablespoon dried oregano
- 1 tablespoon ground cumin
- 1 tablespoon black pepper
- Generous 2 cups (17 fl oz/500 ml) white vinegar
- Juice of 2 lb 4 oz/1 kg oranges
- 6 banana leaves
- 4 pork shanks

To serve:
- 6 Corn Tortillas (page 200)
- Pickled Red Onions (see page 190)
- Lime wedges

This taco sibling of *cochinita pibil* (see page 36) is more common in Mexico City than it is in Yucatán. Here is a combination of sweet orange and white vinegar, though sour orange juice—if you have it on hand—could substitute to provide a very particular flavor. Serve with Pickled Red Onions (see page 190).

Preheat the oven to 400°F/200°C/Gas Mark 6.

Put all the ingredients except the pork, banana leaves, and tortillas in a blender and puree into a sauce.

Layer half of the banana leaves in a baking dish. Add the pork and sauce. Pour in enough water to cover, then top with the remaining banana leaves. Cover with aluminum foil and roast for 3 hours or until very tender. Remove from the oven and chop the meat. Reserve the broth.

TO SERVE
Heat a skillet over high heat for 5 minutes. Add the tortillas, flipping them continuously for 2–3 minutes or until warmed through. Serve the pork on a deep plate with a ladle of the broth over the tortillas and lime wedges on the side.

LIVER TACOS

Prep time: 20 minutes
Cooking time: 30 minutes
Makes: 8

For the liver:
- 10½ oz/300 g beef liver, well washed
- 3 cloves garlic
- 10 dried bay leaves
- 6 sprigs dried thyme
- 6 sprigs dried marjoram
- 1¼ cups (10 fl oz/300 ml) whole (full-fat) milk
- 3 tablespoons olive oil
- 1 white onion, sliced
- Pinch of salt

To serve:
- 8 Corn Tortillas (page 200)
- Lime wedges

One of two versions of beef liver tacos are typically served to children: the first is this comforting stew; the second is liver sautéed with lots of onion and sometimes a bit of serrano chile. Both versions are delicious, though not all kids are convinced of this.

FOR THE LIVER
In a large saucepan, combine the liver, garlic, bay leaves, thyme, marjoram, and milk. Pour in a generous 2 cups (17 fl oz/500 ml) of water. Bring the mixture to a boil over medium–high heat and simmer for 15 minutes or until the liver is very soft, skimming the foam (scum) off the surface of the mixture to prevent it from overflowing. Using a slotted spoon, transfer the liver to a cutting board. Cut into large cubes.

Heat the oil in a skillet over medium heat. Add the onion and sauté for 5 minutes or until the onion is golden. Add the liver and salt and sauté for another 2–3 minutes.

TO SERVE
Heat a skillet over high heat for 5 minutes. Add the tortillas, flipping them continuously for 2–3 minutes or until warmed through. Serve the liver alongside the warmed tortillas, accompanied with lime wedges.

CHORIZO TACOS

Prep time: 30 minutes, plus 2 hours marinating time
Cooking time: 20 minutes
Makes 4

For the green chorizo:
- 2 large bunches spinach, leaves only
- 1 large bunch cilantro (coriander), large stems removed
- 1 small bunch parsley, leaves only
- 3 serrano chiles, stemmed
- 3 tablespoons apple cider vinegar
- 1 tablespoon salt
- 2 lb 4 oz/1 kg ground (minced) pork
- 9 oz/250 g lard
- 1 tablespoon ground cumin
- 1 tablespoon black pepper
- 1 tablespoon ground coriander seeds
- 1 tablespoon ground oregano
- ½ tablespoon ground cloves
- 1 cup (3½ oz/100 g) chopped pumpkin seeds, roasted
- Scant 1 cup (3½ oz/100 g) chopped peanuts, roasted
- Scant 1 cup (3½ oz/100 g) chopped almonds, roasted
- ¾ cup (3½ oz/100 g) raisins
- 2 tablespoons olive oil

To serve:
- 4 Corn Tortillas (page 200)
- ½ white onion, finely chopped
- 10 cilantro leaves, chopped
- 4 lime wedges
- Your choice of sauces (pages 184–97)

In Mexicaltzingo—a town of pork and charcuterie artisan workers in Mexico State—the green chorizo has been perfected. Knowing how to make this delicious chorizo will be an ace up your sleeve for the rest of your life.

FOR THE GREEN CHORIZO
Fill a saucepan three-quarters full of water and bring to a boil over high heat.

Meanwhile, prepare an ice bath by putting a little ice and water in a deep bowl.

When the water begins to boil, add the spinach and herbs separately in batches. Cook each for 2 minutes, then transfer to the bowl with the ice to cool. Transfer the spinach and herbs to a blender. Add the serrano chiles, vinegar, and salt. Blend until smooth.

In a large bowl, combine the meat, lard, spices, pumpkin seeds, nuts, raisins, and spinach mixture. Refrigerate for 2 hours to marinate.

Heat a medium skillet over high heat. Add the olive oil and the marinated meat and cook for 10 minutes or until the meat is cooked through.

TO SERVE
Heat a skillet over high heat for 5 minutes. Add the tortillas, flipping them continuously for 2–3 minutes or until warmed through. Transfer to a plate and top each tortilla with 2–3 tablespoons of green chorizo. Serve with onion, cilantro (coriander), lime wedges, and any of our sauces on the side.

TIJUANA-STYLE GRILLED TACOS

Prep time: 20 minutes, plus 30 minutes marinating time
Cooking time: 15 minutes
Makes: 4

For the adobo pork:
- 10 guajillo chiles, seeded and deveined
- 5 ancho chiles, seeded and deveined
- 2 white onions, diced
- 3 cloves garlic
- Generous 2 cups (17 fl oz/500 ml) white wine vinegar
- 2 tablespoons ground oregano, toasted
- 10 black peppercorns
- ¼ teaspoon salt
- 1 lb 2 oz/500 g pork chop

To serve:
- 4 Corn Tortillas (page 200)
- Guacamole (page 190)
- ½ white onion, finely chopped
- Chopped cilantro (coriander) leaves
- Lime wedges
- Your choice of sauces (pages 184–97)

The *adobada* tacos of Tijuana are close relatives of the *al pastor* tacos of Mexico City. The typical street preparation involves cooking the meat on a vertical spit. Here, we call for grilling, to regain some of the classic Tijuana taquería aroma of smoke and char. In Tijuana, these tacos are served in a tortilla shaped like a cone, with plenty of guacamole. Try it that way.

FOR THE ADOBO PORK
In a saucepan, combine the chiles, onions, and garlic. Add enough water to cover. Bring to a boil and boil for 7 minutes or until the chiles are softened.

Transfer the mixture to a blender. Add the vinegar, oregano, peppercorns, and salt and blend until smooth. In a baking dish, coat the meat well with the marinade. Refrigerate for 30 minutes to marinate.

Preheat a charcoal grill (barbecue) for 10 minutes. Place the pork on the grill over direct heat and grill for 2 minutes on each side or until the meat is cooked through and the exterior looks dark red. Slice thinly and reserve.

TO SERVE
Heat the tortillas on the grill, flipping them continuously for 2–3 minutes or until warmed through. Transfer to a plate and top each tortilla with grilled adobo pork. Serve with guacamole, onion, cilantro (coriander), lime wedges, and any of our sauces on the side.

PORK CHOP TACOS

◐ ◆ ❧ -30

Prep time: 5 minutes
Cooking time: 5 minutes
Makes: 8

- 10½ oz/300 g pork chop
- 2 tablespoons olive oil
- Salt
- Black pepper

To serve:
- 8 Corn Tortillas (page 200)
- ¼ white onion, finely chopped
- Chopped cilantro (coriander) leaves
- 4 lime wedges
- Your choice of sauces (pages 184–97)

At the street-vendor tricycles throughout Mexico City, these tacos are prepared in large batches: the meat is grilled (griddled), chopped, and pushed to the sides of the grill (griddle) until serving time, when a portion is taken from the mountain of meat, put in a tortilla, and handed to the customer. It can be served with raw or roasted onion and cilantro (coriander). This homemade version has the same spirit.

Heat a skillet over high heat for 5 minutes.

Season the pork with salt and pepper. Add the oil and pork to the skillet and cook for 2–3 minutes on each side. Transfer to a cutting board and cut into bite-size cubes.

TO SERVE
Heat a skillet over high heat for 5 minutes. Add the tortillas, flipping them continuously for 2–3 minutes or until warmed through. Transfer to a plate and top each tortilla with pork. Serve with onion, cilantro (coriander), lime wedges, and our sauces on the side.

SONORAN BURRITOS

Prep time: 20 minutes
Cooking time: 15 minutes
Makes: 4

For the meat:
- ¼ tablespoon ground cumin
- ¼ teaspoon salt
- ¼ teaspoon black pepper
- 10½ oz/300 g ground (minced) beef
- 2 tablespoons olive oil

To serve:
- 4 Flour Tortillas (page 201)
- 4 tablespoons Mayonnaise (page 184)
- 4 tomatoes, sliced
- 2 avocados, thinly sliced
- 3½ oz/100 g cooked bacon
- 2 serrano chiles, stemmed and chopped
- 7 oz/200 g Chihuahua cheese
- Your choice of sauces (pages 184–97)

This burrito comes with everything you'd typically find on a food cart in Hermosillo, a city in the north-western state of Sonora. Of course, there are variations on the filling, such as *chilorio* (a Sinaloan pork dish) or machaca (dried meat) with egg, but this is the classic one. To make it *percherón* (a kind of badass size for when you are very hungry; also originally from Sonora), double the size of the tortilla and the quantities of all the ingredients.

FOR THE MEAT
In a bowl, mix the cumin, salt, and pepper. Add the beef and toss to coat with the seasoning.

Heat the oil in a skillet over high heat for 5 minutes. Add the beef and cook for 4–5 minutes, until cooked through.

TO SERVE
Heat a skillet over high heat for 5 minutes. Add the tortillas, flipping them continuously for 2–3 minutes or until warmed through. Transfer to a plate and spread 1 tablespoon of mayonnaise on each tortilla. Top with the meat, tomatoes, sliced avocado, bacon, serrano, and cheese. Fold two opposite sides of the tortilla inward and then roll it into a burrito shape. Return to the pan and pan-fry for 5 minutes or until the cheese is melted.

Place the burritos on a plate, cut in half, and serve with any of our sauces on the side.

CAMPECHANO TACOS

Prep time: 20 minutes
Cooking time: 25 minutes
Makes: 4

- 4 tablespoons olive oil, divided
- 2 white onions, thinly sliced
- 2 tablespoons white wine vinegar
- 1 tablespoon sugar
- 1 lb 2 oz/500 g beef cecina, finely chopped
- 1 lb 2 oz/500 g Green Chorizo (page 90 [chorizo taco]), finely chopped
- 4 Corn Tortillas (page 200)
- 1 lb 2 oz/500 g fried matchstick-cut potatoes
- Lime wedges

The *campechana* aspect of this taco doesn't refer to the city of Campeche, in the Yucatán Peninsula, but to the combination of *cecina*—salted, dried meat—and chorizo. The accent of semi-caramelized onion and fried potatoes are a nod to the center of Mexico.

Heat 2 tablespoons of the olive oil in a skillet over medium heat. Add the onions and sauté for 7 minutes or until the onions begin to change color. Stir in the vinegar and sugar, and simmer over low heat for 5 minutes or until the onions are golden, translucent, and caramelized.

To serve, grease a grill (griddle) with the remaining 2 tablespoons of oil. Add the cecina and chorizo, and sauté for 10 minutes or until they just start to turn golden.

TO SERVE
Heat a skillet over high heat for 5 minutes. Add the tortillas, flipping them continuously for 2–3 minutes or until warmed through. Transfer to a plate and top each tortilla with meat. Serve with the potatoes, caramelized onions, and lime wedges alongside.

BEEF FILLET TACOS

◗ ◗ ☘ *-30*

Prep time: 10 minutes
Cooking time: 5 minutes
Makes: 4

- 4 tablespoons pork lard
- 2 lb 4 oz/1 kg beef fillet, thickly sliced
- Coarse salt

To serve:
- 4 Corn Tortillas (page 200)
- 4 lime wedges
- Your choice of salsa (pages 184–97)

This taco belongs to the tradition of bullring food—though bullrings themselves are fortunately disappearing. Its name is derived from the surname of Rodolfo Gaona, a famous Mexican bullfighter. This taco focuses on the simplicity and tenderness of the meat. Use the best quality of beef possible.

Heat the lard in a grill (griddle) over high heat for 5 minutes.

Generously season the beef with salt. Add the beef to the grill and sear for 4–5 minutes or until golden brown, flipping once. Transfer to a cutting board and let rest for 2 minutes.

TO SERVE
Heat a skillet over high heat for 5 minutes. Add the tortillas, flipping them continuously for 2–3 minutes or until warmed through. Transfer to a plate and top each tortilla with beef. Serve with lime wedges and any of our salsas on the side.

COCHINADA TACOS

Prep time: 10 minutes
Cooking time: 20 minutes
Makes: 4

- 2 tablespoons olive oil
- 7 oz/200 g beef cecina, finely chopped
- 7 oz/200 g Green Chorizo (page 90 [chorizo taco]), finely chopped
- 4 Corn Tortillas (page 200)
- ½ white onion, finely chopped
- Chopped cilantro (coriander) leaves
- ¼ teaspoon salt
- Lime wedges
- Your choice of salsas (pages 184–97), to serve

This taco, the cousin of the *campechano* taco, is known for its topping taquería, the *cochinada*—also known as *cochi* (which literally means "filth")—is collected from the bottom of the chorizo grill after many hours of cooking chorizos. Our approach here is still delicious.

Heat the oil in a medium skillet over medium heat. Add the cecina and chorizo, and sauté for 10 minutes or until they just begin to turn golden. Transfer three-quarters of the mixture to a plate, then cook the remainder of the mixture until it is dark brown, about 5–6 minutes.

TO SERVE
Heat a skillet over high heat for 5 minutes. Add the tortillas, flipping them continuously for 2–3 minutes or until warmed through. Transfer to a plate and top each tortilla with the browned meat mixture, put a spoonful of the "cochinada" on top, and serve with the onion, cilantro (coriander), lime wedges, and any of our salsas on the side.

AL PASTOR TACOS

Prep time: 20 minutes, plus 1 hour
marinating time
Cooking time: 40 minutes
Makes: 4

For the pastor:
- 5 guajillo chiles, seeded and deveined
- 4 tablespoons olive oil, divided
- 3 cloves garlic
- ½ roasted white onion
- ⅔ cup (3½ oz/100 g) achiote paste
- ½ teaspoon ground oregano, toasted
- ½ teaspoon salt
- Pinch of ground cloves, toasted
- Pinch of black pepper, toasted
- Pinch of ground cumin, toasted
- ¼ cup (2 fl oz/60 ml) white wine vinegar
- Juice of 2 oranges
- 10½ oz/300 g pork steak

To serve:
- 4 Corn Tortillas (page 200)
- ¼ white onion, finely chopped
- 3½ oz/100 g grilled pineapple, chopped
- Small bunch cilantro (coriander), coarsely chopped
- 4 lime wedges
- Your choice of sauces (pages 184–97)

Of course, there's something irreplaceable about the huge vertical *pastor* spit in a taquería, the skewered meat roasting laterally as it slowly revolves in front of the fire, gravity helping to shape it. But to cook
at home, simply use a pan over high heat. The marinade is delicate and aromatic.

FOR THE PASTOR
Place the guajillo chiles in a saucepan. Add enough water to cover. Bring to a boil over medium–high heat and boil for 7 minutes or until the chiles are softened. Drain.

Heat 2 tablespoons of the olive oil in a saucepan over medium–low heat. Put all the ingredients except the remaining oil and pork in a blender and blend into a dense paste. Pour the marinade into the saucepan with the hot oil and bring to a boil over high heat. Using a spoon, stir frequently to prevent the mixture from burning and sticking. Simmer for 15 minutes or until the marinade is a dark orange color. Remove from the heat and let cool.

In a large bowl, coat the meat well with the marinade. Refrigerate for 1 hour to marinate.

Heat the remaining 2 tablespoons of oil in a skillet over high heat. Dice the pork, then add it to the skillet and sauté for 7 minutes or until cooked through.

TO SERVE
Heat a skillet over high heat for 5 minutes. Add the tortillas, flipping them continuously for 2–3 minutes or until warmed through. Transfer to a plate and top each tortilla with pork. Serve with onion, pineapple, cilantro (coriander), lime wedges, and any of our sauces on the side.

ARAB TACOS

Prep time: 20 minutes, plus 30 minutes marinating time
Cooking time: 10 minutes
Makes: 4

For the pork filling:
- ½ cup (4 fl oz/120 ml) olive oil, plus 2 tablespoons for frying
- ½ cup (4 fl oz/120 ml) white vinegar
- 1 bunch parsley, leaves only, finely chopped
- 3 tablespoons black pepper
- 2 tablespoons ground oregano
- 1 tablespoon ground clove
- 1 tablespoon ground cumin
- 1 tablespoon garlic powder
- 1 tablespoon dried thyme
- ¼ teaspoon salt
- 1 lb 2 oz/500 g thinly sliced pork chop

To serve:
- 4 pita breads
- 4 lime wedges
- Your choice of sauces (pages 184–97)

The *taco árabe* is one of the great triumphs of migratory cuisines. In the city of Puebla, the meat is roasted on a rotisserie spit fueled by charcoal. At home, you can use a skillet. The addition of harissa is excellent in this taco.

FOR THE PORK FILLING
In a bowl, mix together all the ingredients except the pork.

Place a layer of pork in a small baking dish, then cover it with some of the mixture. Repeat the process, stacking the meat, until all the meat is used up (7–8 layers). Cover and refrigerate for 30 minutes to marinate.

Heat 2 tablespoons of olive oil in a skillet over medium–high heat. Add the pork without removing the marinating mixture and fry for 2–3 minutes on each side, until golden.

TO SERVE
Heat a skillet over high heat for 5 minutes. Add the pitas, flipping them continuously for 3–4 minutes or until warmed through. Place the pita bread on a plate and, using a knife, open the pita pockets and fill with the meat. Serve with lime wedges and any of our sauces on the side.

GREEK TACOS

Prep time: 20 minutes
Cooking time: 35 minutes
Makes: 4

For the pork filling:
- 2 tablespoons olive oil
- 3 white onions, finely chopped
- 10 cloves garlic, finely chopped
- 3 lb 5 oz/1.5 kg mushrooms, thinly sliced
- 2 lb 4 oz/1 kg pork, finely chopped
- ¼ teaspoon ground cloves
- ¼ teaspoon ground cumin
- ¼ teaspoon dried thyme
- ¼ teaspoon salt
- ¼ teaspoon black pepper

To serve:
- 4 Corn Tortillas (page 200)
- ½ white onion, finely chopped
- Chopped cilantro (coriander) leaves
- 4 lime wedges
- Your choice of salsas (pages 184–97)

The charm of this taco lies in its simplicity: grilled mushrooms and pork, garlic and onion, spices ... there is no need to add more. It is a sort of griddle taco to enjoy on any given day.

FOR THE PORK FILLING
Heat the oil in a skillet over medium heat. Add the onion and garlic and sauté for 5 minutes or until golden. Add the mushrooms and sauté for 10 minutes or until the mushrooms have released their moisture and are reduced in size by half.

Add the meat and cloves, cumin, and thyme, and sauté for another 15 minutes, until the pork is cooked through. Season with salt and pepper.

TO SERVE
Heat a skillet over high heat for 5 minutes. Add the tortillas, flipping them continuously for 2–3 minutes or until warmed through. Transfer to a plate and top each tortilla with pork. Serve with onion, cilantro (coriander), lime wedges, and any of our salsas on the side.

PORK AND ONION TACOS

TACOS DE PASTOR
ENCEBOLLADO

Prep time 20 minutes, plus 30 minutes marinating time
Cooking time: 30 minutes
Makes: 4

For the pastor:
- 5 guajillo chiles, seeded and deveined
- ½ cup (3½ oz/100 g) achiote paste
- 3 cloves garlic
- ½ white onion, grilled
- Juice of ½ lime
- ½ teaspoon ground oregano, toasted
- ½ teaspoon salt
- Pinch of ground cloves, toasted
- Pinch of black pepper, toasted
- Pinch of ground cumin, toasted
- Juice of 2 oranges
- ¼ cup (2 fl oz/60 ml) white vinegar
- 2 tablespoons olive oil

For the pork:
- 2 lb 4 oz/1 kg pork steak
- 1 lb 2 oz/500 g white onions, grated
- 2 tablespoons olive oil

To serve:
- 4 Corn Tortillas (page 200)
- ¼ white onion, diced
- 3½ oz/100 g grilled pineapple
- Small bunch cilantro (coriander), coarsely chopped
- 4 lime wedges
- Your choice of salsa (pages 184–97)

This is one of the three great subgenres of the *al pastor* taco, found mainly in Mexico City (see Introduction, page 11). Although the onion component benefits from the pork pressing down on the onion in the spit, we call for a skillet if making the *pastor* at home. So don't skimp on the quantity and intensity of the onion: it's the most important characteristic of this taco.

FOR THE PASTOR
Put the chiles in a saucepan. Add enough water to cover. Bring to a boil over medium–high heat and boil for 7 minutes or until the chiles are softened. Drain.

Place the chiles in a blender. Add all the remaining ingredients except the oil, and blend until smooth. If necessary, add a little water to loosen the mixture.

Heat the oil in a saucepan over high heat. Add the chile mixture and simmer for 5 minutes or until the marinade is a dark red color. Set aside to cool.

FOR THE PORK
In a large bowl, combine the meat, grated onions, and marinade. Refrigerate for 30 minutes to marinate.

Heat the olive oil in a skillet on high heat. Add the marinated meat and onions and sauté for 10 minutes. Slice the steak.

TO SERVE
Heat a skillet over high heat for 5 minutes. Add the tortillas, flipping them continuously for 2–3 minutes or until warmed through. Transfer to a plate and top each tortilla with strips of pork. Serve with onion, pineapple, cilantro (coriander), lime wedges, and any of our salsas on the side.

ROASTED CHICKEN TACOS

Prep time: 20 minutes, plus 1 hour
brining time
Cooking time: 1 hour 15 minutes
Makes: 8

For the brine:
- 3 tablespoons (1¾ oz/50 g) salt

For the chicken:
- 1 whole chicken with skin
  (2 lb 4 oz/1 kg)
- 2 white onions, sliced
- 2 cloves garlic
- 2 tablespoons sugar
- 1 lb 2 oz/500 g melted butter
- Scant 1 cup (7 fl oz/200 ml)
  white vinegar

To serve:
- 8 Corn Tortillas (page 200)
- Caramelized onions
- Guacamole (page 190)
- 4 lime wedges
- Your choice of salsas (pages 184–97)

When you roast a chicken at home, you can take advantage of a 400°F/200°C oven to slowly caramelize the onion. We suggest accompanying these tacos with one of our spicy sauces (pages 184–97) and at least a couple of pickled chiles.

FOR THE BRINE
Mix the salt and 4¼ cups (34 fl oz/1 liter) of water together in a deep bowl.

FOR THE CHICKEN
Place the chicken in the brine and refrigerate for 1 hour. This will help the chicken absorb enough salt during cooking.

Preheat the oven to 400°F/200°C/ Gas Mark 6. Place a wire rack on a baking sheet.

In a saucepan, mix together the onions, garlic, sugar, butter, and vinegar. Heat over medium heat, stirring, for 7 minutes or until everything is well combined.

Place the chicken on the wire rack. Coat with the butter mixture, then cover with aluminum foil and bake for 45 minutes.

Remove the foil and bake for another 20 minutes, basting frequently with the butter mixture.

TO SERVE
Heat a skillet over high heat for 5 minutes. Add the tortillas, flipping them continuously for 2–3 minutes or until warmed through. Place the chicken on a platter. Serve with the tortillas, caramelized onions, guacamole, lime wedges, and any of our salsas on the side.

KEBAB TACOS

Prep time: 20 minutes
Cooking time: 30 minutes
Makes: 4

For the spiced lamb:
- 1 lb 2 oz/500 g ground (minced) lamb
- 10 cloves, ground
- 10 coriander seeds, ground
- 1 tablespoon garlic powder
- 1 tablespoon onion powder
- 1 tablespoon paprika
- 1 teaspoon ground cumin
- ½ tablespoon ground cinnamon
- ½ teaspoon ground nutmeg
- ½ tablespoon salt
- 5 sprigs dill, finely chopped
- 2 tablespoons olive oil

To serve:
- 4 pita breads
- 1 cucumber, thinly sliced
- ½ red cabbage, thinly sliced
- 4 tomatoes, sliced
- Aioli (page 184)
- Your choice of salsas (pages 184–97)

Typically, a kebab is made on a charcoal grill where the heat is always present. The aroma that permeates each "taco" is thanks to years and years of soot, smoke, and endlessly dripping lamb fat over the charcoal. In this homemade version, we make it in a skillet.

FOR THE SPICED LAMB
Combine all the ingredients except the oil in a deep bowl.

Heat the oil in a skillet over high heat. Add the lamb and sauté for 20 minutes, until golden brown.

TO SERVE
Heat a skillet over high heat for 5 minutes. Add the pitas, flipping them continuously for 2–3 minutes or until warmed through. Transfer to a plate and, using a knife, open the pita pockets. Fill with the lamb, cucumber, cabbage, and tomato. Drizzle with aioli and any of our salsas.

COW HEAD TACOS

TACOS DE CABEZA DE RES

Prep time: 20 minutes
Cooking time: 2–3 hours
Makes: 4

For the head meat:
- 1 whole cow head, or 7 oz/200 g in parts, washed thoroughly
- ½ white onion, diced
- 3 cloves garlic
- 10 dried bay leaves
- 6 sprigs dried thyme
- 6 sprigs dried marjoram
- ½ tablespoon salt

To serve:
- 7 oz/200 g cooked Head Meat
- 4 Corn Tortillas (page 200)
- ½ white onion, finely chopped
- 5 sprigs cilantro (coriander), coarsely chopped
- Lime wedges

For this street-style taco, we don't list specific parts of the cow head, but it wouldn't hurt to ask the butcher for a mix: cheek, snout, tongue, maybe a bit of eye if they have it. The possibilities are many.

FOR THE HEAD MEAT
Put all the ingredients in a large saucepan. Add enough water to cover. Bring to a boil, then cover and reduce the heat to medium–low. Simmer for 2–3 hours, until the meat is very tender. (Alternatively, you can use a pressure cooker to halve the cooking time.) Drain the meat, discarding the cooking liquid.

TO SERVE
Heat a skillet over high heat for 5 minutes. Add the tortillas, flipping them continuously for 2–3 minutes or until warmed through. Transfer to a plate, top with the head meat, and garnish with white onion and cilantro (coriander). Serve with lime wedges on the side.

BASKET TACOS

Prep time: 20 minutes
Cooking time: 35 minutes
Makes: 16

For the chicharrón stew:
- 20 guajillo chiles, seeded and deveined
- 1 large white onion, diced
- 6 cloves garlic
- 10 black peppercorns, ground
- 5 cloves, ground
- 3 dried chiles de árbol
- ½ teaspoon ground cumin
- Pinch of salt
- 2 tablespoons olive oil
- 1 lb 2 oz/500 g chicharrones (page 56)

To serve:
- 2 tablespoons olive oil
- 16 Corn Tortillas (page 200)
- Pickled Red Onions (page 190)
- 4 lime wedges
- Your choice of salsa (pages 184–97)

The basket taco belongs to the family of stewed tacos. Here, we use a red salsa pork rind taco—it can be made using our Monterrey-style pork rind recipe (page 56)—but you could also make it using refried beans, potato with chorizo, picadillo, or even *cochinita pibil* (page 36). No matter which you choose to use, the process will be the same.

FOR THE CHICHARRÓN STEW
In a saucepan, combine the chiles, onion, and garlic. Add enough water to cover. Simmer over medium heat for 15 minutes or until the chiles are softened. Drain.

Transfer the mixture to a blender. Add the spices and salt and blend into a smooth sauce.

Heat the oil in a saucepan over medium heat for 5 minutes. Add the pork rinds and three-quarters of the sauce. Simmer for 10 minutes or until the pork rinds have absorbed most of the thickened sauce.

Meanwhile, prepare the serving basket by covering it with a large plastic bag, then lining it with clean dish towels, and then brown kitchen paper, allowing for overhang. All of this will help the tacos retain their heat.

TO SERVE
Preheat a skillet over medium heat for 5 minutes. Add the oil. Dip the tortillas into the chile sauce, removing any excess sauce, and place them in the skillet. Do this in batches, if necessary.

Cook for 1 minute on each side, then transfer to a plate. Top each with the chicharrón stew, fold in half, and place in the basket, wrapping the paper and dish towels over them to keep them warm. Cover with the plastic bag.

Let the tacos rest for 10 minutes, then transfer to a plate. Serve with pickled onions, lime wedges, and any of our salsas.

BRUSSELS SPROUTS TACOS

💧 -30

Prep time: 20 minutes
Cooking time: 10 minutes
Makes: 4

For the spicy peanut butter:
- 3½ oz/100 g peanuts
- 1 tablespoon Aleppo chile powder
- Salt

For the fried Brussels sprouts:
- 4½ cups (34 fl oz/1 liter) vegetable oil
- 20 Brussels sprouts, halved or quartered
- 3 tablespoons mirin
- 2 tablespoons tamari
- 2 tablespoons Yuzu Kosho (page 130)
- 1 tablespoon fish sauce
- Juice of 2 limes, divided
- Salt

For the leek salad:
- 1 young leek, well cleaned, sliced into rings
- 4 tablespoons roasted and chopped peanuts
- 10 cilantro (coriander) leaves, chopped

To serve:
- 4 Corn Tortillas (page 200)
- 1 avocado, pitted and sliced
- 4 lime wedges

When there is less availability of products in the winter, Brussels sprouts work well. Cruciferous vegetables have always been used more as a side than as a main ingredient in Mexico, and the sprouts work very well in tacos when fried. These tacos have a strong spiciness and a tasty amount of fat.

FOR THE SPICY PEANUT BUTTER
Heat the peanuts in a skillet over medium heat, stirring constantly to prevent the peanuts from burning. When the peanuts are hot, transfer them to a blender and blend into a loose paste. Add the Aleppo chile powder and blend again. Season with salt, then set aside in the refrigerator.

FOR THE FRIED BRUSSELS SPROUTS
Heat the vegetable oil in a deep skillet over medium heat.

Meanwhile, fill a saucepan with water, add 2 tablespoons of salt, and bring to a boil over high heat.

Cook the Brussels sprouts in the boiling salted water for 1–2 minutes, until tender, then transfer to the skillet and fry in the hot oil for 4–5 minutes or until golden brown. Transfer to a paper towel–lined plate to drain any excess oil, then place in a deep bowl.

To serve, combine the mirin, tamari, yuzu kosho, fish sauce, and half the lime juice in a small bowl. Pour over the fried sprouts, tossing lightly to coat. Season with salt.

FOR THE LEEK SALAD
Put the leek, peanuts, and cilantro (coriander) in a bowl and season with the remaining lime juice and salt.

TO SERVE
Heat a skillet over high heat for 5 minutes. Add the tortillas, flipping them continuously for 2–3 minutes or until warmed through. Transfer to a plate and spread a spoonful of spicy peanut butter on each tortilla. Top with the fried Brussels sprouts. Serve with the leek salad, slices of avocado, and lime wedges on the side.

SHRIMP TACOS

Prep time: 20 minutes
Cooking time: 20 minutes
Makes: 4

For the marinated shrimp (prawns):
- 10 dried guajillo chiles
- 5 dried ancho chiles
- ½ white onion, coarsely chopped
- 3 cloves garlic
- 2 tablespoons vegetable oil
- 15 raw shrimp (prawns), peeled, deveined, and diced
- 3½ oz/100 g Chihuahua cheese, grated

To serve:
- 4 Corn Tortillas (page 200)
- 4 tablespoons Bean Paste (page 76 [Stew Tacos])
- 3 tablespoons Marinated Shrimp (Prawns)
- ½ white onion, thinly sliced
- 2 serrano chiles, stemmed and thinly sliced into rings
- 6 lettuce leaves, chopped
- Cilantro (coriander) leaves, whole
- 4 lime wedges

This taco is one variation of marinated tacos among many, but it's also the most common one. The dish originates in the lower Pacific region of Mexico (Guerrero), where marinades are widely used. However, the marinade is used in moderation, so it does not overpower the flavor of the main ingredient. I like this taco with either corn or flour tortillas, or a half-flour, half-corn hybrid, which in the Jalisco area is used for birria.

FOR THE MARINATED SHRIMP (PRAWNS)
Put the chiles, onion, and garlic in a saucepan. Add enough water to cover and bring to a boil over medium heat. Simmer for 10 minutes or until the chiles are softened. Drain.

Transfer the onion mixture to a blender and blend into a thick paste.

Preheat a skillet over medium heat. Add the oil, the shrimp (prawns), and the chile paste to the pan. Sauté for 7 minutes or until the mixture just starts to turn a deep red color (or darkens). Sprinkle with the cheese and let it melt.

TO SERVE
Heat a skillet over high heat for 5 minutes. Add the tortillas, flipping them continuously for 2–3 minutes or until warmed through. Transfer to a plate, spread 1 tablespoon of bean paste on each tortilla, then top with cheese-covered shrimp. Top with the onion, serrano chile, lettuce, and cilantro (coriander). Serve with lime wedges on the side.

QUEEN CLAM TOSTADA WITH CHICATANA ANTS

Prep time: 20 minutes
Cooking time: 20 minutes
Makes: 4

For the ant paste:
- 2½ oz/70 g chicatana ants
- 2 tablespoons vegetable oil
- 1 white onion, diced
- 1 habanero chile, quartered
- 1 tablespoon Sriracha
- 2 tablespoons soy sauce
- ½ teaspoon fish sauce
- ½ teaspoon rice vinegar
- ½ tablespoon sesame oil
- 1 tablespoon yuzu juice

For the clam ceviche:
- 12 shelled queen clams, cleaned (chopped)
- 1 cucumber, finely chopped
- 10 chives, finely chopped
- ½ red onion, finely chopped
- 5 cilantro (coriander) stems, finely chopped
- 1 manzano chile, seeded and finely chopped
- Juice of 1 lemon
- 1 tablespoon fish sauce
- 1 tablespoon yuzu juice
- Salt

To serve:
- 4 corn tostadas (You can buy them or bake a tortilla for 10 minutes on 200°F/100°C/Gas Mark ¼ in the oven or until completely dry and crunchy. Let cool for a few minutes.)
- 2 large avocados, sliced
- Cilantro leaves, to garnish
- Your choice of sauces (pages 184–97)

This is in essence a "surf-and-turf" taco. However, instead of meat, we use insects. The strong umami flavor of the ants pairs extremely well with the clams, the earthiness of the ants and the salty freshness of the clams creating a harmonious combination. The combination isn't common, but in Pinotepa Nacional (a city in the state of Oaxaca), it is common to prepare iguanas with chicatana ants. The iguana has a salty freshness similar to that of the clams, which is how we got the inspiration for this taco.

Preheat the oven to 250°F/120°C/Gas Mark ½.

FOR THE ANT PASTE
Place the chicatana ants on a baking sheet lined with parchment paper and heat in the oven for 20 minutes or until the ants are completely dried.

Meanwhile, heat the vegetable oil in a skillet over medium heat. Add the onion and habanero chile. Cook, stirring occasionally, for 10 minutes or until the onion is caramelized.

Transfer the ants and onion mixture to a blender. Add the remaining ingredients and blend into a thick paste.

FOR THE CLAM CEVICHE
Place the clams, cucumber, chives, onion, cilantro (coriander) stems, and manzano chile in a large bowl. Mix together very well, then season with the lemon juice, fish sauce, yuzu, and salt.

TO SERVE
Spread 1 tablespoon of chicatana paste on each tostada. Top each with 4 slices of avocado and 2–3 tablespoons of clam ceviche. Garnish with cilantro leaves and serve with any of our sauces on the side.

OCTOPUS SOPES

Prep time: 20 minutes
Cooking time: 1 hour
Makes: 4

For the octopus:
- 3 tablespoons vegetable oil
- 2 carrots, sliced
- 1 white onion, cut into large cubes
- 3 stalks celery, sliced
- 1 leek, well cleaned, white and light green parts only, sliced into rings
- ¼ teaspoon salt
- 2 lb 4 oz/1 kg octopus tentacles

For the bean puree:
- 9 oz/250 g white beans
- 4 cloves garlic
- Juice of 2 lemons, plus extra to season
- 1 tablespoon sesame oil
- 1 tablespoon habanero oil
- 1 tablespoon garlic oil
- Salt

For the Kalamata olive pico de gallo:
- 10 Kalamata olives, finely chopped
- 1 tomato, seeded and finely chopped
- ½ white onion, finely chopped
- 5 cilantro (coriander) stems, finely chopped
- Lemon juice
- Salt

To serve:
- 4 sopes (use the Corn Tortillas recipe, page 200, but make them ½ inch/1 cm thicker, and pinch the edges to contain the filling)
- 4 tablespoons Bean Puree
- 4 tablespoons Kalamata olive pico de gallo
- Cilantro leaves
- 4 lemon wedges

We are always open to the idea of using other types of beans, such as ayocotes, and also legumes such as chickpeas or peas in recipes; this allows us to play along with the changing of the seasons. In spring, you might use peas, in summer use chickpeas, in the fall (autumn) and winter use beans. You may or may not also use butter, olive oil, or some other type of oil to prepare them.

When cooking octopus, we use relatively large pieces, for texture—the texture is what I like most about octopus. We have made this dish in various ways: with a simple sauce on top, or adding capers (which works very well), or using Chimichurri (page 186) or fresh herbs like coriander, quelite, purslane.

FOR THE OCTOPUS
Heat the oil in a large saucepan over medium heat. Add all the remaining ingredients except the octopus. Add water to fill the pan three-quarters full. Bring to a boil, add the octopus, and simmer, uncovered, for 30 minutes, then turn off the heat, cover, and let stand for 20 minutes.

Drain the octopus, discarding the cooking liquid. Slice the tentacles 2 inches/5 cm thick.

FOR THE BEAN PUREE
Put all the ingredients except the salt into a blender, along with 8½ cups (68 fl oz/2 liters) of water, and blend into a smooth paste. Season with salt and adjust the acidity with lemon juice, if needed.

FOR THE KALAMATA OLIVE PICO DE GALLO
In a deep bowl, toss together the olives, tomatoes, onion, and cilantro (coriander) to mix. Season with lemon juice and salt.

TO SERVE
Heat a skillet over high heat for 5 minutes. Add the sopes, flipping them continuously for 2–3 minutes or until warmed through. Transfer to a plate and spread 1 tablespoon of bean puree on each sope. Sprinkle each with 1 tablespoon of pico de gallo. Top with the octopus tentacles, create a spiral shape starting at the center. Garnish with cilantro leaves and serve with lemon wedges on the side.

TACOS WITH WAGYU, YUZU KOSHO, AND FENNEL FLOWER

TACOS DE WAGYU CROSS, YUZU KOSHO, FLOR DE HINOJO

Prep time: 20 minutes
Cooking time: 15 minutes
Makes: 4

For the yuzu kosho:
- 2 lemons
- 2 limes
- 2 oranges
- 2 grapefruits
- 3½ oz/100 g red fresh serrano chiles, stemmed

For the garlic-thyme oil:
- 1 cup (8 fl oz/250 ml) vegetable oil
- 1 head garlic, cloves separated and finely chopped
- 10 sprigs thyme

To serve:
- 7 oz/200 g Wagyu rib eye
- 4 Corn Tortillas (page 200)
- ¼ teaspoon salt
- Lime wedges
- Fennel flowers, to garnish

Use a high-quality cut of meat for this taco. With tacos, you want a powerful hit of flavor, but many times it can mask the quality of the meat. That's why we've added fennel here, as it allows the elegance of the meat to shine through. If you used a very strong serrano yuzu kosho, there would be no point in using Wagyu. When you have a product of such quality, you have to make sure it stands out.

Preheat a grill (griddle) over high heat for at least 10 minutes.

FOR THE YUZU KOSHO
Zest all the citrus fruits. In a *molcajete* or mortar and pestle, crush the serrano chiles, then add the juice of 1 of the lemons and 1 of the grapefruits and blend into a paste. Stir in the citrus zests and set aside.

FOR THE GARLIC-THYME OIL
Put the oil in a saucepan. Add the garlic and thyme and cook over low heat for 10 minutes. Drain and set aside.

TO SERVE
Grill (griddle) the rib eye for 1–2 minutes per side. Remove from the heat, let rest for 2 minutes and slice into 20 pieces.

Heat the tortillas on the grill, flipping them continuously for 2–3 minutes or until warmed through. Transfer to a plate and spread a small spoonful of yuzu kosho on each tortilla. Top each with 5 pieces of meat. Spoon over 1 tablespoon of garlic oil, add a pinch of salt, and garnish with fennel flowers. Serve with the lime wedges on the side.

FISH FLAUTAS

Prep time: 30 minutes
Cooking time: 40 minutes
Makes: 8

For the machaca sauce:
- 2 tablespoons vegetable oil
- 10 large tomatoes, chopped
- 1 tablespoon grapeseed oil
- 10 guajillo chiles, chopped
- 15 green olives, pitted
- 10 fresh güero chiles
- 6 cloves garlic, finely chopped
- 1 white onion, chopped

For the tuna machaca:
- 4 tablespoons grapeseed oil
- 9 oz/250 g fresh tuna

For the flautas:
- 4½ cups (34 fl oz/1 liter) vegetable oil
- 8 Corn Tortillas (page 200)
- ½ red cabbage, finely sliced
- Lemon juice
- Salt

To serve:
- Cilantro (coriander), to garnish
- 4 tablespoons fresh cream or crème fraîche
- 4 tablespoons crumbled Cotija cheese
- 4 lime wedges
- Your choice of sauces (pages 184–97)

These tacos, made with tuna machaca, are a good way to make use of the fish and avoid waste. They can be made with the leftover meat from other tuna preparations, thus maximizing a quality product.

FOR THE MACHACA SAUCE
Heat the vegetable oil in a skillet over high heat. Add the tomatoes and sauté until they begin to release their juices, about 5 minutes.

Meanwhile, heat the grapeseed oil in another skillet. Add the guajillo chiles and cook until toasted and fragrant, taking care that they do not burn. Stir in the olives, güero chiles, garlic, and onion. Once the mixture starts to caramelize, about 10 minutes, add the sautéed tomatoes. Cook over medium heat for 20 minutes or until the tomatoes darken. Remove from the heat, transfer to a blender, and blend the mixture into a smooth sauce. Set aside.

FOR THE TUNA MACHACA
Heat the oil in a medium skillet over high for 5 minutes. Add the tuna. Using a spoon or spatula (fish slice), flip the fish so that it cooks on both sides. Once the fish begins to turn golden brown, mash it with a spoon so that it falls apart.

Add the machaca sauce, reduce the heat to low, and cook, stirring occasionally, for 10 minutes or until the mixture forms a paste.

FOR THE FLAUTAS
Heat the vegetable oil in a deep fryer or deep saucepan over high heat until it reaches 275°F/140°C. Spoon 2 tablespoons of tuna machaca down the center of each tortilla, then roll tightly into "flutes." Secure the ends with toothpicks (cocktail sticks) to prevent the flautas from unraveling. Carefully lower into the hot oil and deep-fry for 3 minutes or until golden. Using a slotted spoon, transfer to a paper towel–lined plate to drain any excess oil.

Season the cabbage with lemon juice and salt to taste.

TO SERVE
Arrange the flautas on a platter and remove the picks. Top with the cabbage, coriander, a drizzle of cream, and the Cotija cheese. Serve with lime wedges and any of our sauces on the side.

SUADERO TACOS

Prep time: 20 minutes, plus 2 hours
brining time
Cooking time: 2 hours 45 minutes,
plus 45 minutes resting time
Makes: 8

For the suadero:
• ½ cup (3½ oz/100 g) salt
• 1 lb 5 oz/600 g brisket
• 2 tablespoons vegetable oil,
  for greasing
• 1 white onion, diced
• 4 cloves garlic, finely chopped
• 4 ancho chiles, seeded and deveined
• 5 dried bay leaves
• 10 allspice berries

For the radishes:
• 2 radishes, sliced
• ½ red onion, thinly sliced
• Lemon juice
• Salt

To serve:
• 8 Corn Tortillas (page 200)
• 10½ oz/300 g Suadero
• Cilantro (coriander) leaves
• 4 lime wedges
• Your choice of sauces (pages 184–97)

These are perhaps the most popular tacos in Mexico City, made with cuts from the beef belly. Their preparation—slow-cooked, simmering the meat in water and its own fat—makes the meat golden yet juicy and tender. Near Pujol is El Rey del Suadero, a taqueria frequently visited by the restaurant's staff; it is "our corner taqueria," so to speak, and these tacos, of course, are among the most popular.

FOR THE SUADERO
In a large bowl, dissolve the salt in 12¾ cups (3 quarts/3 liters) of water. Add the meat, then refrigerate for 2 hours.

Remove the meat from the brine and pat with paper towels to remove any excess water. Heat the oil in a Dutch oven (casserole) over high heat for 5 minutes. Add the onion and garlic, and sauté for 10 minutes or until the onion is golden brown and caramelized.

Add the meat and sear on all sides, 5–10 minutes per side. Add the chiles, bay leaves, and allspice. Add enough water to cover. Bring to a boil, then reduce the heat to medium, cover, and cook for 20 minutes.

Preheat the oven to 350°F/180°C/Gas Mark 4.

Cook the meat in the oven, covered, for 2 hours. Remove from the oven and let rest in the pot, covered, for 45 minutes.

Cut the meat into large cubes.

FOR THE RADISHES
In a bowl, season the radishes and red onion with lemon juice and salt.

TO SERVE
Heat a skillet over high heat for 5 minutes. Add the tortillas, flipping them continuously for 2–3 minutes or until warmed through. Place the tortillas on a plate and top each with suadero. Top with the dressed radishes and onion, then with the cilantro (coriander). Serve with lime wedges and any of our sauces on the side.

AVOCADO FLAUTAS

◖ ◗ ❧ -30

Prep time: 20 minutes
Cooking time: 10 minutes
Makes: 4

For the crystal shrimp (prawns):
- 9 oz/250 g raw crystal shrimp (prawns), peeled, deveined, and chopped
- 10 cilantro (coriander) leaves
- ¼ cup (1 oz/25 g) finely chopped white onion
- 2 serrano chiles, finely chopped
- Lime juice
- Salt

For the green oil:
- 4 tablespoons vegetable oil
- 3 firmly packed cups (3½ oz/100 g) cilantro

For the chipotle puree:
- 1 1¼ oz/320 g chipotle chiles

For the chipotle mayonnaise:
- 1 egg yolk
- Pinch of salt
- 2 teaspoons lemon juice, divided
- 1 teaspoon Dijon mustard
- 1¼ cups (10 fl oz/300 ml) vegetable oil

To serve:
- 1 avocado, pitted
- 4 tablespoons Chipotle Mayonnaise
- Colima salt
- Zest of 1 lime

These *flautas* were one of Pujol's first gestures toward the world of tacos. Derived from a common homemade dish, stuffed avocados, they evolved at the restaurant until finally culminating in this recipe.

Preheat the oven to 300°F/150°C/ Gas Mark 2.

FOR THE CRYSTAL SHRIMP (PRAWNS)
Place the shrimp in a vacuum bag, seal, and cook in the oven for 5 minutes.

Remove from the oven and let rest, still in the bag.

Remove the shrimp from the bag, cut into medium-sized cubes, then add the cilantro (coriander), onion, and chiles. Season with the lime juice and salt. Set aside.

FOR THE GREEN OIL
Heat the vegetable oil in a deep saucepan over high heat until it reaches 275°F/140°C. Blend the cilantro leaves with the warm oil; strain through a fine-mesh sieve, then pour into a squeeze bottle.

FOR THE CHIPOTLE PUREE
Soak the chiles in hot water for 10 minutes or until softened. Drain. Place the chiles in the (cleaned) blender and, slowly adding scant 1 cup (7 fl oz/200 ml) of water to loosen, blend into a paste. Strain through a fine-mesh sieve and set aside.

FOR THE CHIPOTLE MAYONNAISE
Place the egg yolk in a bowl with a pinch of salt. Using a balloon whisk, beat until emulsified and the salt is dissolved. Slowly add 1 teaspoon of the lemon juice and the mustard, whisking continuously. Pour in the oil in a thin stream, a little at a time, whisking continuously until the mixture has the texture of mayonnaise. Whisk in the chipotle puree and the remaining 1 teaspoon of the lemon juice. Chill in the refrigerator until needed.

TO SERVE
Cut the avocado into long slices.

Spoon the shrimp mixture down the center of a plate. Place the thin avocado slices on top, then roll the edges tightly around to make them into "flute" shapes.

Squeeze a long line of green oil down the center of an oval platter. Arrange the flautas on top of the oil. Place a 2-tablespoon scoop of the chipotle mayonnaise at either end of the line of flautas and sprinkle with salt and lime zest.

FISH CEVICHE TACOS

Prep time: 20 minutes, plus 1 hour marinating time
Cooking time: 5 minutes
Makes: 4

For the marinated fish:
- 1 coconut, flesh coarsely chopped
- Scant ⅔ cup (5 fl oz/140 ml) fresh coconut water
- 1 cup (8 fl oz/250 ml) lime juice
- 1 güero chile
- 2 teaspoons salt
- 4½ oz/120 g white fish (snapper or sea bass), sliced into 12 pieces

To serve:
- 4 Corn Tortillas (page 200)
- 4 slices jicama
- 1 Criollo avocado, pitted and diced
- ¼ red onion, thinly sliced
- 1 güero chile, sliced
- Cilantro (coriander) sprouts, to garnish
- Mint sprouts, to garnish
- Fennel leaves, to garnish

Ceviche in Mexico is a popular dish. It is generally served on a tostada, but to me, the combination of the cold filling and a hot tortilla is delicious.

FOR THE MARINATED FISH
In a blender, blend all the ingredients except the fish. Strain through a fine-mesh sieve into a nonreactive bowl, then add the fish and gently toss to coat. Marinate in the refrigerator for 1 hour.

TO SERVE
Heat a skillet over high heat for 5 minutes. Add the tortillas, flipping them continuously for 2–3 minutes or until warmed through. Transfer to a plate and top each tortilla with a slice of jicama and 3 slices of fish, then add the avocado, red onion, and the sliced güero chile on top. Garnish with cilantro (coriander) sprouts, mint sprouts, and fennel leaves.

KOBE TOSTADAS

Prep time: 30 minutes, plus 24 hours
dehydrating time
Makes: 4

For the Kobe beef tostadas:
- 7 oz/200 g frozen Kobe rib eye
- 4 tablespoons (2 oz/60 g) Colima salt

For the guacamole:
- 2 avocados, pitted
- 1 tablespoon lime juice
- Salt

To serve:
- 1 serrano chile, seeded, deveined, and sliced
- 2 tablespoons thinly sliced scallions (spring onions)
- 4 red cherry tomatoes, halved
- 4 yellow cherry tomatoes, halved
- 4 epazote leave

For this dish, we use the dried meat as the base, as if it were a tostada, then top it with the remaining ingredients. Freeze the rib eye for at least 1 day in advance.

FOR THE KOBE BEEF TOSTADAS
Remove the rib eye from the freezer and slice horizontally into 4 thick slices, then cut each slice into a disk. Place on a baking sheet lined with parchment paper. Sprinkle with the salt and let rest in a dry place, uncovered, for 24 hours to dehydrate.

Remove any excess salt with a clean cloth or brush, and let the beef rest on the parchment paper until it stiffens. Store in an airtight container if not using immediately.

FOR THE GUACAMOLE
Place the avocado in a *molcajete* or mortar and pestle. Add the lime juice, season with salt, and mash into a paste.

TO SERVE
Place the beef tostadas on a plate. Spread 1 tablespoon of guacamole on each tostada, then top each with the serrano chile, scallions (spring onions), 2 red cherry tomato halves, 2 yellow cherry tomato halves, and an epazote leaf.

RABBIT TACOS

TACOS DE
ENTOMATADO
DE CONEJO

◖ ● ❧

Prep time: 20 minutes
Cooking time: 1 hour
Makes: 4

For the hoja santa tortillas:
• ½ cup (2¾ oz/80 g) corn flour masa
• 4 hoja santa leaves

For the rabbit in tomato sauce:
• 4 tablespoons grapeseed oil
• 4 pieces rabbit (14 oz/400 g)
  (we recommend extremities)
• ½ white onion, sliced
• 1 clove garlic, cut into thirds
• 1 Mixe chile
• 3 large tomatoes, cut into eighths
• 15 tomatillos, halved
• 4½ cups (34 fl oz/1 liter) water
• 1 hoja santa leaf
• 1 dried bay leaf
• ½ teaspoon cumin seeds

For the black bean puree:
• 9 oz/250 g black beans, soaked
  overnight and drained
• ½ white onion, chopped
• 2 cloves garlic
• 6 epazote leaves
• ½ cup (approx. 10) avocado
  leaves, toasted
• ¼ teaspoon salt
• Olive oil, for greasing

Entomatados are a Mexican dish of corn tortillas that are covered in a tomato sauce, then filled and topped with other ingredients. They are dishes prepared at home and are something that my mother liked to prepare. If you wanted to replace the protein, you could opt for something soft and neutral, like pork.

FOR THE HOJA SANTA TORTILLAS
Portion the dough into 4 and, using the palms of your hand, roll into balls. Place a ball between 2 pieces of plastic wrap (clingfilm). Using a tortilla press or rolling pin, press on the ball with just enough force to flatten the tortilla. Open the press, peel the plastic wrap off the top of the tortilla, place a hoja santa leaf on the tortilla, cover with the plastic wrap and press again. Using a circle-shaped cookie cutter, trim the edges for a clean outline.

Heat a skillet over medium heat. Place a tortilla in the skillet, and cook for 20 seconds on each side. Remove from the pan and keep warm. Repeat the process with the remaining dough.

FOR THE RABBIT IN TOMATO SAUCE
Heat the oil in a large pot over high heat. Sear the rabbit pieces in the oil for a few minutes until golden brown on both sides. Add the onion and garlic and cook for 10 minutes or until the onion is golden. Add the chile and cook for 2 minutes. Add the tomatoes and tomatillos. Cook for 10 minutes. Add 4½ cups (34 fl oz/1 liter) of water

to the pot and bring to a boil. Add the hoja santa, bay leaf, and cumin. Cook over low heat for 20 minutes or until the rabbit is cooked through.

FOR THE BLACK BEAN PUREE
Place the beans, onion, and garlic in a pot. Add enough water to cover. Cook over medium heat for 30 minutes. Add the epazote leaves, avocado leaves, and salt. Let cool.

Transfer to a blender, then blend until the mixture becomes a smooth paste.

TO SERVE
Place the tortillas on a plate. Top each with the rabbit and tomato sauce, and dot with black bean puree.

ORIGINAL TACOS

143

BARBECUE TACOS WITH CONSOMMÉ

TACOS DE BARBACOA
CON CONSOMÉ

Prep time: 1 hour, plus 3 hours soaking
Cooking time: 4 hours
Makes: 4

For the green tortillas:
- ¾ cup (1 oz/30 g) cilantro (coriander) leaves
- 1 poblano chile, peeled, deveined, and stemmed
- ½ cup (2¾ oz/80 g) corn masa

For the avocado and pea puree:
- 1 avocado, peeled and pitted
- 1 serrano chile
- ¼ white onion, chopped
- ½ firmly packed cup (⅓ oz/10 g) cilantro leaves
- ½ cup (2½ oz/75 g) blanched green peas
- ¼ teaspoon salt

For the barbacoa:
- 3 tablespoons salt
- 1 lb 2 oz/500 g boneless lamb
- 1 maguey leaf
- 1 avocado leaf
- 2 tablespoons vegetable oil

For the consommé:
- 3 large tomatoes, chopped
- 5 dried guajillo chiles, seeded and deveined
- ⅓ cup (2¼ oz/70 g) rice
- 1 hoja santa leaf
- 1 avocado leaf
- Salt

To serve:
- 6 oz/180 g Barbacoa
- Cocoa powder
- 24 sprigs cilantro
- 4 pea tendrils

This is one of the most popular tacos in Mexico. Whether using a pressure cooker or Dutch oven (casserole), cook the meat as slowly as possible, in its own juices. The juices are delicious and should always be served on the side.

FOR THE GREEN TORTILLAS
In a blender, puree the cilantro (coriander) with the poblano chile. If necessary, add 1 tablespoon of water to loosen. Pass through a fine-mesh sieve. Mix with the masa and knead until completely mixed.

Portion the dough into 4 and, using the palms of your hand, roll into balls. Place a ball between 2 pieces of plastic wrap (clingfilm). Using a tortilla press or rolling pin, press on the ball with just enough force to flatten the tortilla. Open the press, and peel the plastic wrap off the top of the tortilla. Using a circle-shaped cookie cutter, trim the edges for a clean outline.

Heat a skillet over medium heat. Place a tortilla in the skillet and cook for 20 seconds on each side. Remove from the pan and keep warm. Repeat the process with the remaining dough.

FOR THE AVOCADO AND PEA PUREE
In the (clean) blender, puree all the ingredients except the salt. Season with salt, then pass the puree through a fine-mesh sieve. Pour into a squeeze bottle.

FOR THE BARBACOA
Heat a Dutch oven (casserole) over medium heat. Add 3 cups (25 fl oz/750 ml) of water and salt, stirring to dissolve the salt. Place the lamb in the water with a maguey leaf and avocado leaf, remove from the heat, and soak for 3 hours. Drain, reserving the cooking broth.

Debone the meat without tearing it. Divide the lamb into 4 portions.

Heat the oil in a skillet over high heat. Sear the meat in the hot oil for 5 minutes just before serving.

FOR THE CONSOMMÉ
Put the tomatoes, guajillo chiles, reserved barbacoa cooking broth, and rice in a large saucepan. Cook, covered, over medium heat for 1 hour. If necessary, add a little water to prevent the mixture from drying out.

Transfer the mixture to a blender and blend until smooth. Strain through a fine-mesh strainer into the pot.

Stir in the hoja santa and avocado leaves. Season with salt. Remove and discard the leaves before serving.

TO SERVE
Place the green tortillas on an oval platter. Top each with the barbacoa and avocado and pea puree. Sprinkle with the cocoa, and garnish each with 6 cilantro sprigs and 1 pea tendril. Pour the hot consommé into a small pitcher (jug), for drizzling over the tacos when serving.

ORIGINAL TACOS

GRILLED ONION TACOS

TACOS DE
CEBOLLA ASADA

Prep time: 10 minutes
Cooking time: 40 minutes
Makes: 4

For the onion petals:
• 1 white onion

For the escamoles:
• 1½ tablespoons butter
• 2 teaspoons olive oil
• 2 tablespoons white onion, diced
• 1 clove garlic, finely chopped
• 1 serrano chile, diced
• 7 oz/200 g escamoles
• 5 epazote leaves, finely chopped
• ¼ teaspoon salt

To serve:
• 4 large Onion Petals
• Epazote sprouts

Since escamoles come from the earth, I like to serve them with ingredients that grow underground, such as leeks, onions, turnips—two ingredients found in the same place prepared together. Onion especially is commonly used when preparing escamoles, and the combination works very well.

Preheat the oven to 350°F/180°C/ Gas Mark 4.

FOR THE ONION PETALS
Wrap the onion in aluminum foil and bake for 40 minutes. Remove the aluminum foil, cut the onion in half, and, when it's cool enough to handle, separate the petals. Reserve the 4 largest ones. (The remaining petals can be used in other recipes.)

FOR THE ESCAMOLES
Heat a skillet over high heat for 2–3 minutes. Add the butter and olive oil. Add the onion, garlic, and chile, and sauté for 2–3 minutes, until the onion has softened. Stir in the escamoles and remove from the heat. Add the epazote and season with salt.

TO SERVE
Place the onion petals on an oval platter. Fill each with the escamoles, and garnish with epazote sprouts.

CHICHILO TACOS

Prep time: 1 hour 30 minutes
Cooking time: 1 hour
Makes: 4

For the parsnip puree:
- 9 oz/250 g parsnips, diced
- Generous 2 cups (17 fl oz/500 ml) heavy (double) cream
- 1 teaspoon salt

For the turkey breast:
- 6 oz/180 g skinless, boneless turkey breast
- 3 tablespoons butter
- 2 tablespoons clarified butter
- Salt

For the black chichilo sauce:
- 10 dried black chilhuacle chiles, seeded and deveined
- 2 dried pasilla de Oaxaca chiles, seeded and deveined
- 1 white onion, sliced
- 7 oz/200 g green tomatoes
- 10½ oz/300 g roma tomatoes
- 2 corn tostadas (You can buy them or bake a tortilla for 10 minutes on 200°F/100°C/Gas Mark ¼ in the oven or until completely dry and crunchy. Let cool for a few minutes.)
- 2 cloves garlic
- 2 cloves
- 4 black peppercorns
- 1 tablespoon dried thyme
- ¼ teaspoon cumin seeds
- 1 tablespoon dried oregano
- ¼ teaspoon dried marjoram
- 50 g lard
- 1 oz/25 g dough for Corn Tortillas (page 200)
- 1 avocado leaf
- ¼ teaspoon salt

To serve:
- 4 Corn Tortillas (page 200)
- 4 tablespoons Parsnip Puree
- Dried thyme, toasted until darkened
- Dried marjoram, toasted until darkened
- Cilantro (coriander) sprouts
- 1½ cups (12 fl oz/350 ml) Black Chichilo Sauce

Chichilo negro is a traditional celebration dish, one of the most emblematic moles of Mexico, yet new to the world of tacos. Serve these tacos immediately, before the tortillas get soggy and break. Parsnip has a sweet flavor, with the same profile as chichilo, and pairs well with it in this taco.

FOR THE PARSNIP PUREE
Heat the parsnip with the cream and salt in a saucepan. Cook over medium heat for 15 minutes or until the parsnip has softened. Transfer to a blender and blend until smooth. Strain through a fine-mesh sieve. Set aside.

FOR THE TURKEY BREAST
Preheat the oven to 150°F/65°C. Season the turkey breast with salt and place in a vacuum bag with the 3 tablespoons of butter. Seal the bag. Cook in the oven for 30 minutes. Remove from the oven and let rest in the bag for 10 minutes. Remove from the bag and cut into 4 slices. When ready to serve, heat the clarified butter in a skillet over medium–high heat. Add the turkey and sear on both sides, 3–5 minutes per side.

FOR THE BLACK CHICHILO SAUCE
Roast the chiles on a grill (griddle) over medium heat until they acquire a slight black color, then transfer them to a bowl of hot water and let soak for 15 minutes.

Meanwhile, roast the garlic, onion, and tomatoes on the grill. Toast the tortillas on the grill until they are almost blackened on both sides. Once toasted, soak the tostadas in a bowl of warm water for 5 minutes.

In a blender, blend the garlic, onion, spices, and herbs with 1 cup (8 fl oz/250 ml) of water. Remove to a bowl and set aside.

In a (clean) blender, blend the chiles and tortillas into a thick paste.

Heat the lard in a saucepan over high heat. Add the blended spice mixture and then the chile-tortilla mixture. Reduce the heat to medium and cook, stirring constantly, for 8 minutes.

Dissolve the tortilla dough in 1 cup (8 fl oz/250 ml) of cold water and add to the previous mixture; stir to incorporate. Add the roasted tomatoes and cook, covered, for 8 minutes or until softened.

Char the avocado leaf on the grill over direct heat and add it to the saucepan. Season with salt.

Transfer the mixture to the blender and blend until smooth. Strain through a fine-mesh sieve.

TO SERVE
Place the tortillas on an oval platter. Spoon parsnip puree in a line down the center of each. Place a slice of turkey on top of the puree, then sprinkle with the thyme and marjoram and garnish with the coriander sprouts. Pour the black chichilo sauce into a small pitcher (jug), for drizzling over the tacos when serving.

SEA BASS TATAKI AL PASTOR

TACOS DE TATAKI DE ROBALO AL PASTOR

Prep time: 15 minutes, plus 1 hour marinating time
Cooking time: 20 minutes
Makes: 4

For the marinated bass:
- 6 dried guajillo chiles
- 4 cloves garlic, chopped
- 13 oz/375 g chopped roma tomatoes
- ½ white onion, chopped
- 10 oz/280 g bass loin
- Salt

For the garden mix:
- ¼ white onion, diced
- 1 serrano chile, diced
- Lemon juice
- ¼ teaspoon salt

To serve:
- 4 Corn Tortillas (page 200)
- 4 tablespoons pineapple puree
- Lemon juice
- Cilantro (coriander) sprouts

This was one of our first tacos. The idea is to let the fish shine on its own. We suggest using a slightly fatty fish, so the flavor stands out. *Kampachi* or *hamachi* (both yellowtail tunas), sea bass … any cold-water fish that stands up to marinade and pineapple will work.

FOR THE MARINATED BASS
To a pot over low heat, add a generous ½ cup (4¼ fl oz/125 ml) of water, along with the guajillo chiles, garlic, tomatoes, and onion. Cook for 15 minutes or until the ingredients are softened. Season with salt.

Remove the marinade from the heat and let cool, then transfer to a blender and blend until smooth. Pour into a shallow dish and add the bass loin, turning to coat well. Refrigerate for 1 hour to marinate. Remove from the marinade and cut into 12 very thin slices.

FOR THE GARDEN MIX
In a bowl, mix together the onion and chile. Season with lemon juice and salt.

TO SERVE
Heat a skillet over high heat for 5 minutes. Add the tortillas, flipping them continuously for 2–3 minutes or until warmed through. Transfer to an oval platter. Spread each with pineapple puree, then top each with 3 slices of marinated bass. Top the fish with garden mix and finish with a few drops of lemon juice and cilantro (coriander) sprouts.

SEA URCHIN TACOS

Prep time: 40 minutes
Cooking time: 20 minutes
Makes: 4

For the tomato paste (puree):
- 9 oz/250 g tomatoes, diced
- 1 clove garlic
- ¼ white onion, chopped
- ¾ cup (½ oz/15 g) cilantro (coriander) leaves
- ¼ teaspoon salt

For the poblano vinaigrette:
- Scant 1 cup (7 fl oz/200 ml) vegetable oil
- 7 oz/200 g poblano chile
- Scant ½ cup (3½ fl oz/100 ml) olive oil
- ⅓ cup (1¾ oz/50 g) white onion, diced
- ¼ teaspoon salt
- ⅔ cup (5 fl oz/150 ml) lemon juice, strained

To serve:
- 2 sea urchin tongues, halved
- 4 Flour Tortillas (page 201)
- 2½ tablespoons Tomato Paste (Puree)
- ½ avocado, peeled, pitted and sliced
- Sliced scallion (spring onion)
- ½ serrano chile, sliced
- Cilantro (coriander) sprouts

This was an early exploration of the tacos at Pujol. The sea urchin has an intense, distinctive flavor. We use a flour tortilla, like the tacos prepared in Baja California, and we serve it with ingredients that accompany but do not overshadow or contrast its flavor—avocado, tomato, and poblano vinaigrette.

FOR THE TOMATO PASTE (PUREE)
Cook the tomatoes, garlic, and onion in a skillet over medium heat for 15 minutes or until fully softened. Transfer to a blender and blend along with the cilantro (coriander) and salt, then strain through a fine-mesh sieve. Reserve the paste and the liquid separately.

FOR THE POBLANO VINAIGRETTE
Prepare an ice bath by putting a little ice and water in a container. Heat the vegetable oil in a skillet over medium–high heat. Add the poblano chile and blanch until the skin loosens. Remove from the oil and cool in the ice bath, then remove the seeds and veins, and dice into small cubes. Set aside.

In the skillet, heat the olive oil over low heat. Add the onion and sauté for 2–3 minutes or until caramelized. Add the poblano chile and salt. Cook for 3 minutes, then stir in the reserved liquid from the tomato paste (puree). Remove from the heat and let cool. Stir in the lemon juice, then set aside.

TO SERVE
Place the sea urchin tongues on a baking sheet and char with a blow-torch on one side only.

Heat a skillet over high heat for 5 minutes. Add the tortillas, flipping them continuously for 2–3 minutes or until warmed through. Transfer to an oval platter. Spread each tortilla with tomato paste, then drizzle with poblano vinaigrette. Top with a slice of avocado and a piece of sea urchin tongue. Garnish with scallion (spring onion), chile slices, and cilantro sprouts.

QUESILLO-STUFFED CUARESMEÑO CHILES

TACOS DE CUARESMEÑOS RELLENOS DE QUESILLO

Prep time: 35 minutes
Cooking time: 25 minutes
Makes: 8

- 4 cuaresmeño chiles
- 10½ oz/300 g quesillo cheese (Oaxaca cheese), shredded
- Salsa Martajada (page 172), optional
- 8 Corn Tortillas (page 200)

The cuaresmeño is a docile chile in terms of heat—there are some brave ones, but in general they are mild chiles. It is a variant of jalapeño; the fruit is cut once it has ripened on the bush. This taco makes for a tasty snack, and the combination of chiles and cheese is well known, but the quesillo cheese adds a special touch.

Preheat a grill (barbecue) over high heat.

Place the chiles on the grill and roast over a high flame for 5 minutes or until charred, using tongs to rotate them so that they char evenly. Transfer them to a plastic bag, then wrap the bag with a dish towel. Let the chiles rest for 5–10 minutes. The steam in the bag will finish cooking the chiles and loosening the skins. Remove from the bag and peel off the charred skin. (Do not rinse the chiles with running water or they will lose their flavor.) Make a length-wise cut from the top of each chile and remove the seeds and veins. Do not remove the stems, as it keeps the chiles intact.

Stuff the chiles with the cheese. Place them on a baking sheet. Bake them as they are, or first pour some of the sauce over the top.

Cook for 10 minutes or until the filling is very hot and the sauce (if using) is bubbling.

Warm the (remaining) sauce in a saucepan over medium heat. Heat a skillet over high heat for 5 minutes. Add the tortillas, flipping them continuously for 2–3 minutes or until warmed through. Place the stuffed chiles in a deep plate and pour the warmed sauce over them. Serve with the tortillas on the side.

PORK BELLY AND RED BEAN TACOS

TACOS DE PANZA
DE CERDO, ALUBIAS
AHUMADAS,
VERDOLAGAS

◗ ◗ ❧

Prep time: 35 minutes, plus
12 hours soaking time
Cooking time: 1 hour, plus
13 hours steaming time
Makes: 8

For the pork belly:
• 1 cup (8½ oz/240 g) salt
• 1 lb 2 oz/500 g pork belly, skin removed
• 4 large cloves garlic
• 1 cup (8 fl oz/250 ml) olive oil

For the bean puree:
• 4¼ oz/120 g dried white beans
• 1 teaspoon salt
• 1 teaspoon lemon juice
• 1 teaspoon olive oil

For the smoked beans:
• 4¼ oz/120 g cooked white beans
• 1 teaspoon salt
• ¾ oz/20 g mesquite wood chips
• 5 avocado leaves
• 5 guava leaves

For the avocado sauce:
• 1 avocado, peeled and pitted
• 4 sprigs cilantro (coriander)
• ½ serrano chile, finely chopped
• Juice of 1 lime
• Salt

For the grilled cucumber:
• 4 cucumber slices

For the purslane salad:
• 4¼ oz/120 g Smoked Beans
• 3½ oz/100 g purslane
• 2 radishes, thinly sliced
• ¼ red onion, finely chopped
• 4 tablespoons Avocado Sauce
• Pinch of salt

To serve:
• 1 tablespoon vegetable oil
• 8 Corn Tortillas (page 200)

The combination of flavors and textures in this taco makes it special: the tenderness of the pork belly with its golden crust, the smokiness of the beans, the fresh and crunchy purslane salad, the creaminess of the bean puree, and the essential complement of the avocado.

FOR THE PORK BELLY
In a large bowl, dissolve the salt in 8½ cups (68 fl oz/2 liters) of water and soak the pork belly for 1 hour. Drain.

Preheat the oven to 150°F/65°C with steam (at home you can place the bags in a deep saucepan and add enough water to cover). Place the pork in a vacuum bag measuring 10 × 14 inches/25 × 35 cm, along with the garlic and olive oil. Seal the bag and cook for 13 hours. Transfer to a bowl of ice and a cup of water to cool, then remove the pork from the bag and cut into 3 oz/90 g pieces.

FOR THE BEAN PUREE
Soak the beans in a generous 2 cups (17 fl oz/500 ml) of water for 12 hours. Drain, then cook over medium heat in a pot with salted water for 30 minutes or until softened. Drain, reserving some of the cooking liquid. Let the beans cool, then transfer to a blender and blend with the lemon juice, olive oil, and a few tablespoons of the cooking liquid into a smooth puree. If necessary, add more cooking liquid to loosen. Pass the mixture through a fine-mesh sieve, put in a piping bag or dispenser bottle, and refrigerate until ready to use.

FOR THE SMOKED BEANS
Soak the beans in a generous 2 cups (17 fl oz/500 ml) of water for 12 hours. Drain, then cook in a large saucepan over medium heat with 34 fl oz/1 liter of water and a pinch of salt for 30 minutes or until softened. Drain and transfer to a perforated baking sheet.

Put the wood chips in a saucepan, add the avocado and guava leaves, and set over a fire. Once the chips ignite, cover the pan with a lid. Place the baking sheet with the beans

in the oven on the middle rack and place the pan with the chips and leaves, uncovered, at the bottom. Smoke the pork at 85°F/30°C for 15 minutes. Remove from the oven and set aside.

FOR THE AVOCADO SAUCE
In a *molcajete* or mortar and pestle, grind the avocado pulp with the cilantro and chile. Mix in the lime juice and season with salt.

FOR THE GRILLED CUCUMBERGrill the 4 cucumber slices on a grill (griddle) over high heat.

FOR THE PURSLANE SALAD
In a bowl, toss all the ingredients.

TO SERVE
In a skillet over medium–high heat, cook 4 pieces of pork belly, fat-side down, for 7 minutes, until golden brown and caramelized. Transfer to a plate. Pipe a disk of bean puree next to the pork. Make a cavity in the center of the puree and fill it with the oil. Serve with grilled cucumber, purslane salad, and tortillas on the side.

POTATO AND CHEESE FLAUTAS

Prep time: 35 minutes
Cooking time: 45 minutes
Makes: 12

For the flautas:
- 1 lb 2 oz/500 g yellow potatoes
- 1 lb 2 oz/500 g quesillo cheese (Oaxaca cheese), shredded
- ½ cup (4 oz/115 g) fresh cream or crème fraîche
- 4½ cups (34 fl oz/1 liter) vegetable oil
- 12 Corn Tortillas (page 200)
- Salt

To serve:
- ½ cup (4 oz/115 g) fresh cream or crème fraîche
- 1 cup (4 oz/125 g) crumbled queso fresco
- ½ lettuce, chopped
- Your choice of sauces (pages 184–97)

Flautas are a very common dish in Mexico. They are an everyday kind of food. The cheese gives elasticity to the taco—a very pleasant sensation when eating it. The idea of this recipe is to maintain that homemade feeling of the dish.

Preheat the oven to 375°F/190°C/Gas Mark 5.

FOR THE FLAUTAS
Place the potatoes on a baking sheet and bake for 30 minutes or until the potatoes are softened and can be easily pierced with a knife.

Mash the potatoes with their skins, then stir in the cheese and cream in a bowl. Season with salt.

Heat the oil in a large skillet over high heat until very hot but not smoking (350°F/180°C). Spoon 2 tablespoons of the potato mixture down the center of each tortilla, then roll tightly into "flutes." Secure the ends with toothpicks (cocktail sticks) to prevent the flautas from unraveling. Make 12 flautas. Carefully lower into the hot oil and deep-fry for 3 minutes or until golden and crispy. Using a slotted spoon, transfer to a paper towel–lined plate to drain any excess oil.

TO SERVE
Arrange the flautas on a platter and remove the picks. Serve with cream, fresh queso fresco, lettuce, and any of our sauces on the side.

SUADERO AND TURNIP TACOS

Prep time: 1 hour, plus 1 hour
brining time
Cooking time: 2 hours 15 minutes
Makes: 4

For the short rib suadero:
- ¼ cup (1¾ oz/50 g) Colima salt
- 1 lb 5 oz/600 g bone-in short ribs
- 7 oz/200 g lard, divided
- 1 carrot, sliced
- 1 large white onion, diced
- 3 cloves garlic, finely chopped
- 4 avocado leaves

For the turnip puree:
- 3¼ oz/90 g turnip, peeled and diced
- 2 scallion (spring onion) bulbs, finely chopped
- Lime juice
- Salt

To serve:
- 4 Corn Tortillas (page 200)
- 4 teaspoons Turnip Puree
- ¼ white onion, finely diced
- Cilantro (coriander) leaves
- 4 lime wedges

Shabu-shabu—a Japanese meat and vegetable hotpot dish—is typically served with plenty of grated turnip. It was a reference and inspiration for this taco.

FOR THE SHORT RIB SUADERO
In a deep bowl, dissolve the salt in 12¾ cups (3 quarts/3 liters) of water. Place the meat in the brine and refrigerate for 1 hour.

Heat a large saucepan over high heat for 5 minutes. Add half of the lard, let it melt, then add the ribs, searing on all sides until golden brown. Add the carrot, onion, and garlic, and cook for 10 minutes or until softened. Remove from the heat and set aside.

Preheat the oven to 210°F/100°C.

Place the meat with the vegetables in a large ovenproof dish, add enough water to cover, add the avocado leaves, cover tightly, and cook in the oven for 1 hour 30 minutes.

Drain the meat, reserving the cooking liquid, then remove and discard the bones. Dice the suadero.

Melt the remaining lard in a medium saucepan over medium heat. Add all the cooking liquid from the suadero and bring to a boil. Add the suadero to the pan and cook for 20 minutes, stirring occasionally. Drain the meat and set aside.

FOR THE TURNIP PUREE
Blend the turnip in a blender until smooth; drain through a fine-mesh sieve. Place in a bowl, mix with the scallion (spring onion), and season with lime juice and salt. Set aside.

TO SERVE
Heat a skillet over high heat for 5 minutes. Add the tortillas, flipping them continuously for 2–3 minutes or until warmed through. Transfer to a plate and top each tortilla with 2–3 tablespoons of hot suadero. Top with a dollop of turnip puree. Serve with onion, cilantro (coriander), and lime wedges on the side.

EGGS AND GREEN BEANS TACOS

TACOS DE HUEVO
CON EJOTES

Prep time: 1 hour
Cooking time: 45 minutes
Makes: 8

For the green beans:
• 5½ oz/160 g green beans
• 2 tablespoons olive oil

For the caramelized onion:
• 2 tablespoons vegetable oil
• 12 pearl onions
• ½ teaspoon sugar
• 1 tablespoon white wine

For the tortilla powder:
• 3 Corn Tortillas (page 200)

For the perfect egg yolks:
• 4 fresh eggs
• ¼ teaspoon salt

To serve:
• 8 Corn Tortillas (page 200)
• Cilantro (coriander) sprouts
• Colima salt
• Olive oil

Egg with green beans is a common breakfast in Mexican homes. It reminds me of a taco sold in my elementary school, which came with a cascabel chili sauce. It's a childhood memory I treasure with affection—and that I have a deep craving for.

FOR THE GREEN BEANS
Bring a saucepan three-quarters full of salted water to a boil. Add the green beans and blanch for 6 minutes. Meanwhile, prepare an ice bath by putting a little ice and water in a deep container. Drain the beans, then stop the cooking process by placing them in the ice bath.

Once the beans are cold, drain and transfer to a bowl. Toss with the oil.

FOR THE CARAMELIZED ONION
Heat the oil in a saucepan over medium heat. Add the onions, sugar, and wine. Cook for 10 minutes, stirring, or until the onion has softened and caramelized.

FOR THE TORTILLA POWDER
Preheat the oven to 275°F/140°C/Gas Mark 1. Place the tortillas on a baking sheet lined with parchment paper and bake for 25 minutes. Let cool, then transfer to a blender and grind into fine powder.

FOR THE PERFECT EGG YOLKS
Fill a saucepan three-quarters full of salted water and bring to a boil over high heat. Carefully add the eggs. Reduce the heat to 150°F/65°C and cook uncovered for 16 minutes, keeping the water at that temperature.

Carefully remove the eggs from the water and let cool for 5 minutes.

Peel the shells by lightly cracking each egg at the slender end. Separate the egg white from the yolk. (The whites can be used in other recipes.)

TO SERVE
Heat a skillet over high heat for 5 minutes. Add the tortillas, flipping them continuously for 2–3 minutes or until warmed through. Transfer to a plate and top each tortilla with the egg yolk, a handful of green beans, the caramelized onions on the side of the beans and sprinkle with tortilla powder, garnish with cilantro (coriander) sprouts. Finish with a sprinkle of salt and a drizzle of olive oil.

TEMPURA FISH TACOS

Prep time: 3 hours, plus 12 hours marinating time
Cooking time: 1 hour 20 minutes
Makes: 4

For the tempura batter:
- ⅓ cups (5 oz/160 g) potato starch
- 2 cups (1 lb 2 oz/500) g all-purpose (plain) flour
- 3 tablespoons salt
- 4½ cups (34 fl oz/1 liter) sparkling (mineral) water

For the miso mayonnaise:
- 1 egg yolk
- Generous 2 cups (17 fl oz/500 ml) canola (rapeseed) oil

- 4 tablespoons white miso
- Zest and juice of 1 lemon
- 1 tablespoon tamari
- Salt

For the tamarind miso:
- 5½ oz/150 g tamarind pulp
- 4 tablespoons white miso
- ½ tablespoon piloncillo
- 2 tablespoons guajillo chile powder

For the miso coleslaw:
- Scant 1 cup (7 fl oz/200 ml) rice vinegar
- 2 tablespoons mirin
- 1 teaspoon sugar
- ¼ teaspoon salt
- 3½ oz/100 g white cabbage, cut into strips

- 3½ oz/100 g red cabbage, cut into strips
- 1 cup (7 oz/200 g) Miso Mayonnaise
- 2 tablespoons Tamarind Miso

To serve:
- 4½ cups (34 fl oz/1 liter) vegetable oil
- 4 pieces (11¼ oz/320 g) mahi mahi fish
- 1 carrot, cut into matchsticks
- ½ red onion, julienned
- Lemon juice
- 4 Flour Tortillas (page 201)
- 4 tablespoons Tamarind Miso
- 8 tablespoons Miso Coleslaw
- Cilantro (coriander) leaves
- 2 serrano chiles, seeded, deveined, and cut into matchsticks
- Salt

A version of the fish tacos typical of the northern part of the country, with a special flavor added by tamarind miso: a very distinctive touch of acidity.

FOR THE TEMPURA BATTER
In a bowl, mix together the potato starch, flour, and salt with a whisk. Add the mineral water in 2 parts, mixing constantly until the ingredients form a homogeneous mixture. Keep in the refrigerator until needed.

FOR THE MISO MAYONNAISE
Put the egg yolk in a deep bowl and, whisking continuously with a balloon whisk, slowly pour in the oil in a steady stream. Whisk in the miso, lemon zest and juice and tamari until well mixed. Season with salt. Keep in the refrigerator until needed.

FOR THE TAMARIND MISO
Put the tamarind pulp, miso, and piloncillo in a saucepan over medium–high heat. Pour in 1¼ cups (10 fl oz/300 ml) of water. Using a silicone spatula, scrape the bottom of the pan occasionally to prevent sticking. Once the mixture begins to boil, reduce the heat to low, add the guajillo chile powder, and cook for 1 hour or until the mixture has reduced by three-quarters. Remove from the heat, cool, and then refrigerate until needed.

FOR THE MISO COLESLAW
In a large bowl, mix together the rice vinegar, mirin, sugar, and salt. Add both types of cabbage, tossing to coat. Marinate in the refrigerator for 12 hours. Drain the mixture very well and return to the bowl. Toss with the miso mayonnaise and tamarind miso to coat well. Set aside.

TO SERVE
Heat the oil in a large saucepan over medium heat. Using tongs, dip the fish (cold, from the fridge) in the tempura batter, then carefully lower into the hot oil. Cook for 5 minutes or until the mixture is golden. Transfer to a paper towel–lined plate to drain any excess oil.

Season the carrot and onion with lemon juice and salt.

Heat a skillet over high heat for 5 minutes. Add the tortillas, flipping them continuously for 2–3 minutes or until warmed through. Transfer to a plate and top each tortilla with a piece of fish, 1 tablespoon of tamarind miso, and 2 tablespoons of coleslaw. Garnish with the dressed carrot and onion, and cilantro (coriander) leaves.

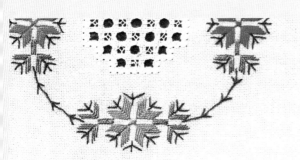

LOBSTER GRINGAS

Prep time: 30 minutes
Cooking time: 40 minutes
Makes: 8

For the lobster:
- 1 lb 9 oz/700 g lobster tail
- 3 tablespoons butter, divided
- Salt

For the guajillo marinade:
- 15 guajillo chiles
- 4 tablespoons pumpkin seed oil
- ¼ white onion, diced
- 3 cloves garlic
- Salt

To serve:
- 8 Flour Tortillas (page 201)
- 1 oz/25 g Edam cheese, shredded
- Thin pineapple sticks
- ½ white onion, finely chopped
- Lemon juice
- Olive oil
- 12 cilantro (coriander) leaves
- Lime wedges
- Salt

Lobster is delicious on its own, and the combination with adobo, cheese, and flour tortillas enhances its flavor. It is a reimagining of the classic gringas found in taquerias: al pastor meat and cheese in flour tortillas.

FOR THE LOBSTER
Clean the lobster tail by removing the shell from the meat. Cut it in half lengthwise, remove the intestine, and rinse the meat under running water. Drain and pat very dry with paper towels.

Place each half of the lobster tail meat in a vacuum bag measuring 5 × 7 inches/12.5 × 17.5 cm with 1½ tablespoons of the butter. Sprinkle with salt, then seal the bags.

Preheat the oven to 250°F/120°C/ Gas Mark ½ with steam (at home you can place the bags in a deep saucepan and add enough water to cover) and cook for 20 minutes.

FOR THE GUAJILLO MARINADE
Put the chiles in a saucepan and add enough water to cover. Cook over medium heat for 2 minutes or until the chiles are softened. Drain.

Heat the oil in a skillet over medium heat. Add the onion, garlic, and chiles and sauté for 5 minutes or until softened. Season with salt, then remove from the heat. Transfer the mixture to a blender and blend into a smooth paste.

Remove the lobster meat from the bags, and cut each piece in half lengthwise. Using a paring knife, make 5 horizontal slits in the top of each, being careful to not cut through the meat completely. Using a brush, spread the guajillo marinade over the lobster.

TO SERVE
Preheat the oven to 325°C/160°C/ Gas Mark 3.

Heat a skillet over high heat for 5 minutes. Add the tortillas, flipping them continuously for 2 minutes or until warmed through. Transfer to a baking sheet and top 4 of the tortillas with 1 piece of lobster each. Sprinkle with the cheese, then put in the oven for 2–3 minutes, until the cheese is melted.

In a bowl, dress the pineapple and onion with lemon juice, olive oil, and salt to taste.

Place the lobster tortillas on a plate and top with the pineapple mixture. Add the cilantro (coriander) leaves, top with another tortilla to cover, and serve with lime wedges on the side.

SOFT SHELL CRAB AND KALE TACOS

TACOS DE JAIBA
DE CONCHA SUAVE

Prep time: 20 minutes
Cooking time: 45 minutes
Makes: 4

For the sikil pak:
- 5 tomatoes, halved
- ¼ white onion, chopped
- 2 cloves garlic
- 1 habanero chile
- ¼ cup (1¼ oz/35 g) almonds
- 3 tablespoons pumpkin seeds
- 3 tablespoons olive oil
- Pinch of salt

For the XO sauce:
- 3½ tablespoons vegetable oil
- 6 mulato chiles, chopped
- 20 cloves garlic, cut into thin chips
- 2-inch (5 cm) piece of ginger
- 3 tablespoons coriander seeds, toasted
- ½ cup (3½ oz/100 g) roasted peanuts

For the macadamia puree:
- ½ cup (3½ oz/100 g) macadamia nuts
- 2 cloves garlic
- Juice of 1 lime
- 2 tablespoons vegetable oil
- Salt

For the crispy crabs:
- 2 cups (17 fl oz/500 ml) vegetable oil
- 2 soft-shell crabs
- 1 cup (6 oz/175 g) katakuriko (potato starch)

To serve:
- 4 Corn Tortillas (page 200) (we recommend pink corn)
- 4 tablespoons Macadamia Puree
- 4 tablespoons Sikil Pak
- ¼ white onion, julienned
- 4 whole medium kale leaves (we recommend soaking in hot salted water for 2 minutes first), each cut into a circle

This taco, topped with a tangy cabbage salad and lime is typical of Baja California. It has a flavor profile similar to that of *chil-pachole*, a Mexican soup traditionally made with crab or prawns. Here, the soft crab is very subtly seasoned, and the raw cabbage provides texture and acidity. We also prepare it with shiso.

Preheat the oven to 350°F/180°C/ Gas Mark 4.

FOR THE SIKIL PAK
In a deep bowl, toss the tomatoes, onion, garlic, chile, almonds, and pumpkin seeds with the olive oil and salt to coat. Transfer to a baking sheet and bake for 20 minutes or until the tomatoes are golden brown. In a blender, blend the tomatoes, onion, garlic, and chile, then add the almonds and seeds and blend into a smooth puree.

FOR THE XO SAUCE
Heat the vegetable oil in a small skillet over medium heat. Add the mulato chiles to the hot oil, turn off the heat, and stir constantly so that the chiles brown but don't burn, about 5 minutes. Add the garlic and ginger to the oil over low heat and fry for 3–4 minutes or until browned.

Using a spider or slotted spoon, transfer the garlic chips to a paper towel–lined plate to drain any excess oil. In a blender, blend the garlic, ginger, and mulato chiles with the remaining cooking oil, coriander seeds, and peanuts into an oily sauce with bits.

FOR THE MACADAMIA PUREE
In a (clean) blender, blend the macadamia nuts, garlic, lime juice, and vegetable oil into a smooth paste. If necessary, add a little water to loosen. This should take about 10 minutes. Season with salt.

FOR THE CRISPY CRAB
Heat the vegetable oil in a saucepan over medium heat. Halve the crabs horizontally. Coat each crab half with the katakuriko (potato starch). Deep-fry the crabs for 5 minutes or until they just begin to turn golden brown. Transfer to a paper towel–lined plate to drain any excess oil. Set aside.

TO SERVE
Heat a skillet over high heat for 5 minutes. Add the tortillas, flipping them continuously for 2–3 minutes or until warmed through. Transfer to a plate and spoon 1 tablespoon of macadamia puree in the center of each tortilla and, right next to it, 1 tablespoon of sikil pak. Top with a piece of crispy crab, and garnish with the julienned onion and a circle of kale. Serve with XO sauce on the side.

FISH CHORIZO TACOS

Prep time: 30 minutes
Cooking time: 1 hour
Makes: 4

For the lemon, habanero, and garlic oils:
- 8 tablespoons vegetable oil, divided
- Zest or peel of 1 lemon (avoid the pith)
- 1 tablespoon dried habanero chiles
- 2 cloves garlic

For the chorizo marinade:
- 2 tablespoons olive oil
- ½ white onion, diced
- 2 cloves garlic, diced

- 3 tomatoes, diced
- ½ cup (3½ oz/100 g) macadamia nuts
- 6 mulato chiles, chopped
- 6 ancho chiles, chopped
- 10 sprigs dried thyme, toasted
- 4 cloves, toasted
- ½ teaspoon cumin seeds, toasted
- ½ teaspoon black pepper, toasted
- ½ teaspoon ground oregano, toasted

For the fish chorizo:
- 2 tablespoons olive oil
- 7 oz/200 g tuna, finely chopped
- ½ white onion, finely chopped

- 10 cilantro (coriander) leaves, finely chopped
- 2 tablespoons Lemon Oil
- 2 tablespoons Habanero Oil
- Pinch of salt

To serve:
- 1 white onion, peeled
- 4 Corn Tortillas (page 200) (we recommend pink corn)
- 4 tablespoons Garlic Oil
- 4 cilantro (coriander) leaves
- Green tomato salsa, to serve (pages 191, 193, 194, and 195)

This was one of the first tacos we made at Pujol, with the idea of using the entire fish. At the restaurant, "chorizo" is made from the fish, and onion is roasted and then used as a casing of sorts for the fish chorizo. Finally, the tortilla embraces the onion, forming a "nigiri." The taco is visually very clean, because all the filling is inside the onion. This taco is a good reminder to us chefs that we always have to remember how tacos are eaten: if they are served too full, they cannot be closed; if the sauce is added first, the tortilla breaks. In this case, the taco is easy to handle, all the ingredients are contained, and it can be eaten in a couple of bites.

FOR THE LEMON, HABANERO, AND GARLIC OILS
In a saucepan over medium heat, heat 2 tablespoons of the oil to 210°F/100°C, for about 8 minutes. Remove from the heat and add the lemon zest. Let stand in the oil and put in the fridge to cool. Repeat the process with the habanero chiles and then the garlic with the remaining 4 tablespoons of oil.

FOR THE CHORIZO MARINADE
Heat the olive oil in a saucepan over medium heat for 5 minutes. Add the onion, garlic, and tomatoes. Cook, stirring, for 10 minutes or until the tomatoes have released their juices. Add the macadamia nuts, chiles, herbs, and spices. Cook for 10 minutes or until the chiles are softened (if necessary, add a little water).

Transfer the mixture to a blender and blend into a smooth marinade. Set aside.

FOR THE FISH CHORIZO
Heat the olive oil in a skillet over medium heat for 5 minutes. Add the fish and chorizo marinade. Cook for 15 minutes, stirring continuously to avoid sticking. Remove the fish

chorizo from the heat, then mix in the onion, cilantro (coriander), lemon oil, habanero oil, and salt. Set aside to cool.

TO SERVE
Preheat the oven to 350°F/180°C/ Gas Mark 4.

Using a grill (barbecue) or the stove over direct heat, burn the onion until the outside layer is completely blackened. Let stand for 10 minutes, then bake in the oven for 5 minutes. Remove from the oven and trim off the ends. Cut the onion in half lengthwise, remove the core, and separate the large outer layers.

Heat a skillet over high heat for 5 minutes. Add the tortillas, flipping them continuously for 2–3 minutes or until warmed through. Transfer to a plate.

Stuff 4 large onion layers with 2 tablespoons of chorizo each, top with 1 tablespoon of the garlic oil and a cilantro leaf, and fold into an oval shape. Place each onion package (parcel) on a tortilla and serve with green salsa on the side.

ORIGINAL TACOS

SEARED TUNA TACOS, SHISO, SALSA MARTAJADA

TACOS DE ATÚN SELLADO, SHISO, SALSA MARTAJADA

Prep time: 15 minutes, plus 3 hours marinating time
Cooking time: 30 minutes
Makes: 4

For the seared tuna:
- 10½ oz/300 g tuna
- Scant 1 cup (7 fl oz/200 ml) soy sauce
- 3 serrano chiles, stemmed and finely chopped
- 4 tablespoons (7 oz/200 g) chili powder
- 2 tablespoons olive oil

For the salsa de vena with chintextle:
- 2 tablespoons olive oil, divided
- ½ white onion, cut into large cubes
- 2 cloves garlic
- 4 tomatoes, cut into large cubes
- Veins and seeds of 7 fresh chiles (serrano, jalapeño, habanero, etc.)
- 1 tablespoon chintextle
- 2 tablespoons rice vinegar
- 1 tablespoon white soy sauce

To serve:
- 4 Corn Tortillas (page 200) (we recommend white corn)
- 4 tablespoons Salsa de Vena with Chintextle
- 4 shiso leaves

If you want to prepare tacos where the tuna stands out, this is the recipe. It is simple to make, but it is delicious.

FOR THE SEARED TUNA
Place the tuna, soy sauce, and chiles in a deep bowl. Turn the tuna in the marinade to coat. Marinate in the refrigerator for 3 hours.

FOR THE SALSA DE VENA WITH CHINTEXTLE
Heat 1 tablespoon of the oil in a saucepan over medium heat for 5 minutes. Add the onion, garlic, tomatoes, and chili veins and seeds. Cook for 10 minutes or until the tomatoes have released their juices.

Transfer the mixture to a blender and add the chintextle, vinegar, remaining 1 tablespoon of the oil, and white soy sauce. Blend in short intervals, to ensure that the sauce has a crushed consistency.

TO SERVE
Remove the tuna from the marinade and pat with paper towels to remove any excess soy sauce. Coat the tuna on all sides with the chili powder.

Heat the oil in a skillet over medium–high heat. Add the tuna and, sear on each side in 1-minute intervals for 2–3 minutes. Remove from the pan and let rest for 2 minutes, then slice into 4 medallions.

Heat a skillet over high heat for 5 minutes. Add the tortillas, flipping them continuously for 2–3 minutes or until warmed through. Transfer to a plate and top each tortilla with a tuna medallion and 1 tablespoon of salsa de vena. Garnish with a shiso leaf.

SCALLOP TACOS

Prep time: 30 minutes, plus 1 hour marinating time
Cooking time: 5 minutes
Makes: 4

- 1 cup (2 oz/55 g) sugar
- 1 cup (2 oz/55 g) Colima salt
- 1½ cups (3½ oz/100 g) finely chopped cilantro (coriander)
- 1½ cups (3½ oz/100 g) finely chopped mint
- 4 large hatchet scallops
- 1 large avocado, peeled and pitted
- 4 Corn Tortillas (page 200) (we recommend black corn)

- 1 tablespoon yuzu kosho (page 130 [Wagyu, Yuzu kosho, and Fennel Flower Tacos])
- 12 slices pickled ginger
- 4 shiso leaves
- 10 cilantro leaves
- Your choice of sauces (pages 184–97)

This taco was inspired by Japanese culinary traditions. The Japanese usually do not include external elements in their cuisine. It is usually simpler than Mexican cuisine, which integrates the ingredients more. Both approaches have their charm.

Combine the sugar, salt, chopped cilantro (coriander), and mint in a deep bowl. Gently coat the scallops with the mixture and let stand for 1 hour in the refrigerator.

Remove the scallops from the mixture, removing any excess with a little water, and pat dry well with paper towels.

Cut the avocado and scallop into 12 thin slices.

Heat a skillet over high heat for 5 minutes. Add the tortillas, flipping them continuously for 2–3 minutes or until warmed through. Transfer to a plate and spread each tortilla with yuzu kosho. Top each with 1 slice of avocado, 1 slice of scallop, 1 slice of ginger. Repeat the process until you have 3 layers. Top with a shiso leaf and the cilantro leaves. Serve with any of our sauces on the side.

CHICKEN CHICHARRÓN TACOS

◑ ◊ ❧

Prep time: 20 minutes
Cooking time: 45 minutes
Makes: 4

For the avocado puree:
- ¼ white onion, diced
- 1 clove garlic
- 1 serrano chile
- 10 sprigs cilantro (coriander)
- 1 large avocado, peeled and pitted
- Juice of 2 lemons
- Salt

For the salsa de vena:
- 2 tablespoons olive oil
- ½ white onion, diced
- 2 cloves garlic, cut into cubes
- 4 tomatoes, cut into large cubes
- Veins and seeds of 7 fresh chiles
  (serrano, jalapeño, habanero, etc.)

For the chicken chicharrón:
- 8 pieces chicken skin (approx.
  3 x 3 inches)
- 4½ cups (34 fl oz/1 liter) vegetable oil

To serve:
- 4 Corn Tortillas (page 200)
  (we recommend yellow corn)
- 4 tablespoons Avocado Puree
- 4 tablespoons Pico de Gallo (page 191)

This is a version of a *taco placero*, the *botana* taco, the quintessential Mexican appetizer, which uses chicken skin instead of pork rinds. Chicken skin is almost never consumed by itself in Mexico, and we began using it with the idea of taking advantage of the entire chicken. Although really, for this taco, any chicharrón works—pork, fish, even beef.

FOR THE AVOCADO PUREE
In a blender, blend the onion, garlic, serrano chile, and cilantro (coriander) for 2 minutes, then add the avocado and puree. Stir in the lemon juice. Season with salt.

FOR THE SALSA DE VENA
Heat the oil in a saucepan over medium heat for 5 minutes. Add the onion, garlic, tomatoes, and chile veins and seeds. Cook for 10 minutes or until the tomatoes have released their juices. Transfer the mixture to a blender and, pulsing the motor, puree the mixture until the sauce is a crushed consistency.

FOR THE CHICKEN CHICHARRÓN
Preheat the oven to 250°F/120°C/ Gas Mark ½.

Carefully skim off as much fat from the chicken skin as possible. Place the skins, fat-side down, on a baking sheet lined with parchment paper and let dry in the oven for 20 minutes.

Heat the vegetable oil in a deep saucepan over medium heat until it reaches 275°F/140°C.

Carefully lower the chicken skins into the hot oil and deep-fry until crispy— this doesn't take long, only seconds, so do not let them burn.

TO SERVE
Heat a skillet over high heat for 5 minutes. Add the tortillas, flipping them continuously for 2–3 minutes or until warmed through. Transfer to a plate and top each tortilla with 1 tablespoon of avocado puree, 2 pieces of chicken chicharrón, and 1 tablespoon of pico de gallo. Serve with salsa de vena on the side.

ORIGINAL TACOS

OCTOPUS-STUFFED CHILE TACOS

Prep time: 15 minutes
Cooking time: 45 minutes
Makes: 4

For the octopus with chintextle:
- 2 tablespoons chintextle
- 2 tablespoons red miso
- 1¼ cups (10 fl oz/300 ml) olive oil
- 1 lb 2 oz/500 g whole cooked octopus

For the fried chickpeas:
- 16 cooked chickpeas
- Scant 1 cup (7 fl oz/200 ml) vegetable oil

For the bean hummus:
- 1 lb 2 oz/500 g cooked white beans
- 2 cloves garlic
- Juice of 2 lemons
- Scant ½ cup (3½ fl oz/100 ml) olive oil
- Salt

To serve:
- 4 güero chiles, roasted and deveined
- 4 Corn Tortillas (page 200) (we recommend white corn)
- 4 tablespoons Bean Hummus
- ¼ white onion, sliced
- Cilantro (coriander) leaves
- 4 lime wedges

The idea of this taco is similar to that of our Fish Chorizo Taco (page 170), where a separate dish is placed on top of tortillas. Other chiles can be substituted for the güeros (cuaresmeños or dried chiles, for example), just take care that they are not too spicy. As well, the protein—as with most tacos—can vary: use whatever protein you want. This versatility is one of the inherent characteristics of tacos.

FOR THE OCTOPUS WITH CHINTEXTLE
Preheat a grill (griddle) over high heat for 10 minutes.

In a bowl, mix together the chintextle and miso. Stir in the olive oil. Add the octopus and gently toss to coat with the marinade. Place the octopus on the grill and cook for 2–3 minutes on each side. Remove from the heat and cut into small cubes.

FOR THE FRIED CHICKPEAS
Preheat the oven to 250°F/120°C/Gas Mark ½.

Place the chickpeas on a baking sheet lined with parchment paper and dehydrate in the oven for 20 minutes or until the chickpeas are completely dry.

Heat the vegetable oil in a deep saucepan until it reaches 275°F/140°C. Carefully lower the chickpeas into the hot oil and deep-fry—this doesn't take long, only seconds, so do not let them burn.

FOR THE BEAN HUMMUS
Put the beans, garlic, and lemon juice in a blender and blend into a very smooth paste for about 10 minutes. Season with salt.

TO SERVE
Stuff the chiles with the chopped octopus and set aside.

Heat a skillet over high heat for 5 minutes. Add the tortillas, flipping them continuously for 2–3 minutes or until warmed through. Transfer to a plate and top each tortilla with 1 tablespoon of bean hummus, a stuffed chile, 4 fried chickpeas, sliced onion, and cilantro (coriander) leaves. Serve with lime wedges on the side.

GREEN BEAN AND PEANUT TACOS

TACOS DE EJOTES CON ENCACAHUATADO

Prep time: 15 minutes
Cooking time: 45 minutes
Makes: 4

For the green bean bundles:
- 2 tablespoons salt
- 32 green beans
- 12 chives

For the encacahuatado:
- 2 tablespoons vegetable oil
- 1 white onion, diced
- 3 cloves garlic
- 6 tomatoes, diced
- 1 ripe plantain, sliced
- Scant 1 cup (5½ oz/150 g) toasted peanuts
- 2 dried chiles de árbol
- 6 guajillo chiles
- 1 small piece ginger (1 inch/2.5 cm)
- 3 cloves garlic
- ½ teaspoon cumin seeds, toasted
- 4 allspice berries
- 1 habanero chile, stemmed
- Salt

To serve:
- 4 Corn Tortillas (page 200) (we recommend yellow corn)
- 4 tablespoons Encacahuatado
- Your choice of sauces (pages 184–97), to serve

This taco is more of an appetizer than a main. In Mexico, vegetable tacos are not very common, and green beans specifically are typically used only in stews. But we think that vegetable tacos are a good option. The peanuts here provide protein. *Encacahuatados*—moreish sauces, can vary widely in terms of texture, spiciness, and the types of seeds used.

FOR THE GREEN BEAN BUNDLES
Half-fill a saucepan with water, add the salt, and bring to a boil over high heat. Meanwhile, prepare an ice bath by putting a little ice and water in a deep container. Cook the beans in the hot water for 2 minutes or until they are a deep green color. Transfer them to the ice bath to stop the cooking. Repeat the process with the chives—though they will take only a few seconds to cook.

Place 8 cooked green beans crosswise on top of 3 chives. Use the chives to tie up the green beans, making sure that they are very well secured. Repeat to make 3 more bundles.

FOR THE ENCACAHUATADO
Heat the oil in a saucepan over medium heat. Add the onion, garlic, tomatoes, and plantain. Cook for 10 minutes or until the tomatoes have released their juices. Season with salt. Add the remaining ingredients and cook for 10 more minutes.

Transfer the mixture to a blender and blend into a thick but very smooth paste. Return to the saucepan and cook over medium heat for 10 more minutes, stirring occasionally to prevent it from burning.

TO SERVE
Heat a skillet over high heat for 5 minutes. Add the tortillas, flipping them continuously for 2–3 minutes or until warmed through. Transfer to a plate and spread 1 tablespoon of encacahuatado on each tortilla. Top with a bundle of green beans. Serve with any of our sauces on the side.

SALSAS

CREAMY SAUCES

MAYONNAISE

MAYONESA

Prep time: 20 minutes
Makes: Scant 1 cup (7 fl oz/200 ml)

- 1 egg yolk
- Pinch of salt
- Scant 1 cup (7 fl oz/200 ml) vegetable oil
- Juice of 2 lemons

Fill three-quarters of a metal bowl with ice. Line it with a dish towel, then place another metal bowl on top.

Add the egg yolk and salt to the top bowl. Using a balloon whisk, whisk until the mixture begins to resemble a thick paste. Pour in the oil in a slow, thin, steady stream, whisking continuously. It's important to add the oil a little at a time, otherwise

the mayonnaise may separate and turn lumpy. Add 3 tablespoons of water halfway through the process to stabilize the mayonnaise.

To finish, stir in the lemon juice.

The mayonnaise can be stored in an airtight container in the refrigerator for up to 1 week.

AIOLI

ALIOLI

Prep time: 10 minutes
Makes: Scant 1 cup (7 fl oz/200 ml)

- 1 egg yolk
- 2 cloves garlic, finely chopped
- Pinch of salt, plus extra to season
- Scant 1 cup (7 fl oz/200 ml) vegetable oil
- Juice of 3–4 lemons

There are two ways to make aioli. The simplest method is to use a hand mixer to blend all the ingredients, not moving the mixer until the mixture begins to emulsify, then moving the mixer slowly until the oil is fully incorporated. The second method is similar to that for making mayonnaise (see above), only you make a paste with the garlic, and you can use a *molcajete* or mortar and pestle.

In a bowl, combine the egg yolk, garlic, and salt. Using a balloon whisk, beat into a thick and pale-yellow

paste. Slowly pour in the oil in a slow, steady stream, whisking continuously. It's important to add the oil a little at a time, otherwise the aioli may split and turn lumpy. To prevent the aioli from splitting, add 3 tablespoons of water halfway through the process to stabilize the aioli.

Season with the lemon juice and more salt to taste.

The aioli can be stored in an airtight container in the refrigerator for up to 1 week.

GUACACHILE

GUACACHILE

ï ⱴ ◖ ◢ ✿ -30

Prep time: 10 minutes
Cooking time: 20 minutes
Makes: Scant 1 cup (7 fl oz/200 ml)

- 10 serrano chiles, stemmed
- 4 cloves garlic
- 2 white onions, quartered
  and layers separated
- Scant 1 cup (7 fl oz/200 ml)
  vegetable oil
- Juice of 1 lime
- Pinch of salt

Heat a saucepan over low heat. Combine the chiles, garlic, and onions in the pan. Pour in the oil and cook for 20 minutes or until the onion is translucent. Using a slotted spoon, transfer the solid ingredients to a blender and blend until smooth. Add the lime juice and salt. (The flavorful chili oil can be reserved for use in other recipes.)

The guacachile can be stored in an airtight container in the refrigerator for up to 1 week.

OIL-BASED SALSAS

SALSA MACHA

SALSA MACHA

ï ⱴ ◢ ✿ -30

Prep time: 5 minutes
Cooking time: 7 minutes
Makes: Scant 1 cup (7 fl oz/200 ml)

- Scant 1 cup (7 fl oz/200 ml)
  vegetable oil
- 10 ancho chiles
- 10 guajillo chiles
- 10 chiles de arbol
- 10 cloves garlic
- ⅔ cup (3½ oz/100 g) peanuts, toasted
- Scant ½ cup (3½ oz/100 g) sesame
  seeds, toasted
- ½ teaspoon salt

In a saucepan, heat half of the oil over medium heat for 5 minutes. Add the chiles, garlic, peanuts, and sesame seeds, and stir continuously with a wooden spoon for 2–3 minutes or until the chiles change to a golden color and are softened.

Transfer the mixture to a blender and blend with the remaining oil. Stir in the salt.

The salsa can be stored in an airtight container in the refrigerator for up to 3 weeks.

CHIMICHURRI

CHIMICHURRI

ï   v   ●   ◐   ❧   -30

Prep time: 5 minutes, plus 2 hours
marinating time
Makes: Scant 1 cup (7 fl oz/200 ml)

- 10 tender sprigs oregano,
  finely chopped
- 4 cloves garlic, finely chopped
- 1 small green chile, finely chopped
- 1 bunch parsley, finely chopped
- Scant ½ cup (3½ fl oz/100 ml) olive oil
- 3 tablespoons grape or balsamic vinegar
- Juice of 2 lemons
- ¼ teaspoon salt
- ¼ teaspoon black pepper

Combine all the ingredients in
a glass bowl. Let stand for 2 hours.

The chimichurri can be stored
in an airtight container in the refrigerator for up to 2 weeks.

HARISSA

HARISSA

ï   v   ●   ◐   ❧   -30

Prep time: 15 minutes, plus 12 hours
marinating time
Makes: Scant 1 cup (7 fl oz/200 ml)

- 3 cloves garlic
- Scant 1 cup (3½ oz/100 g) hot paprika
- Scant ½ cup (1¾ oz/50 g) sweet paprika
- ½ tablespoon coriander seeds, toasted
- ½ tablespoon cumin seeds, toasted
- ¼ tablespoon caraway seeds, toasted
- ¼ teaspoon salt, plus extra to season
- 1 cup (8 fl oz/240 ml) olive oil

In a food processor, combine all the
ingredients and process into a smooth
paste. Season with salt, then refrigerate for 12 hours to intensify the flavors.

The harissa can be stored in an
airtight container in the refrigerator
for up to 2 weeks.

FERMENTED SAUCES AND VINEGARS

CHILTEPÍN SAUCE

SALSA DE CHILTEPÍN

Ï ν ◖ ◗ ❧ -30

Prep time: 15 minutes
Cooking time: 10 minutes
Makes: 1¼ cups (10 fl oz/300 ml)

• 10 dried chiltepín chiles, toasted
• 2 tomatoes, chopped
• 2 cloves garlic, chopped
• ½ white onion, halved
• ½ teaspoon ground oregano, toasted
• ¼ teaspoon ground cumin, toasted
• ¼ teaspoon coriander seeds, toasted
• ½ cup (4 fl oz/120 ml) white vinegar
• 1 tablespoon olive oil
• Pinch of salt

In a saucepan, combine the chiles, tomatoes, garlic, onion, oregano, and spices. Add enough water to cover. Bring to a boil over high heat, then boil for 10 minutes or until the tomatoes are softened. Drain.

Transfer the mixture to a blender. Add the vinegar, and blend until smooth.

Heat the oil in a skillet over low heat. Pour in the chile mixture, increase the heat to medium, and bring the mixture to a boil. Stir in the salt and remove from the heat.

The sauce can be stored in an airtight container in the refrigerator for up to 1 week.

YUCATECAN HABANERO SAUCE

SALSA YUCATECA DE HABANERO

Ï ν ◖ ◗ ❧ -30

Prep time: 5 minutes
Makes: 1¼ cups (10 fl oz/300 ml)

• 10 habanero chiles, stemmed
• 4 cloves garlic
• 1 white onion, chopped
• ¼ teaspoon cumin seeds, toasted
• ¼ teaspoon ground oregano, toasted
• ½ cup (4 fl oz/120 ml) bitter orange juice (you can substitute with regular orange juice, but add a little vinegar, i.e., ¼ cup/2 fl oz/60 ml each juice and vinegar)
• Pinch of salt

Put all the ingredients in a blender and blend until smooth.

The sauce can be stored in an airtight container in the refrigerator for up to 1 week.

BAJÍO-STYLE SAUCE

SALSA TIPO BAJÍO

Prep time: 15 minutes
Cooking time: 5 minutes
Makes: 1¼ cups (10 fl oz/300 ml)

- 8 dried chiles de árbol, stemmed
- 15 piquín chiles
- 4 cloves roasted garlic
- ¼ cup (2 fl oz/60 ml) white vinegar
- ¼ teaspoon ground cumin, toasted
- ½ teaspoon ground oregano, toasted
- ¼ teaspoon black pepper, toasted
- Pinch of salt
- 1 tablespoon olive oil

Place the chiles in a small saucepan and add enough water to cover. Cook over medium–high heat for 10 minutes or until the chiles are softened. Drain.

Transfer the chiles to a blender. Add all the remaining ingredients except the salt and oil and blend until smooth.

Heat the oil in a skillet over medium–high heat. Add the chile mixture and salt. Stir, using a wooden spoon, then bring to a boil. When the sauce reaches the boil, remove from the heat.

The sauce can be stored in an airtight container in the refrigerator for up to 2 weeks.

CHAPULINE RED SAUCE

SALSA ROJA CON CHAPULÍN

Prep time: 15 minutes
Cooking time: 10 minutes
Makes: 1¼ cups (10 fl oz/300 ml)

- 10 large whole tomatoes
- ½ white onion, chopped
- 3 cloves garlic
- 3 dried chiles de árbol, stemmed
- 3½ oz/100 g grasshoppers (chapulines), toasted
- ¼ teaspoon salt

Heat two skillets over low heat. In one of the skillets, combine the tomatoes, onion, and garlic over medium–high heat. Cook, stirring occasionally, for 10 minutes or until the onion is golden.

Meanwhile, put the chiles in the second skillet and add a little water. Simmer over medium heat for 5 minutes or until the chiles are softened. Drain.

Transfer the tomato mixture and chiles to a blender. Add the grass-hoppers and blend until smooth. If necessary, add a little water to loosen the mixture, taking care not to make the sauce too watery. Season with the salt, to taste.

The sauce can be stored in an airtight container in the refrigerator for up to 3 days.

CHICATANA ANT SAUCE

SALSA DE HORMIGA CHICATANA

◗ ◖ ♦ ❧ -30

Prep time: 5 minutes
Cooking time: 10 minutes
Makes: 1¼ cups (10 fl oz/300 ml)

- 10 large whole tomatoes
- ½ white onion, chopped
- 3 cloves garlic
- 3 dried chiles de árbol, stemmed
- 3½ oz/100 g chicatana ants, toasted
- Salt

Heat two skillets over low heat.

In one of the skillets, place the tomatoes, onion, and garlic over medium–high heat and cook for 10 minutes or until golden.

Meanwhile, put the chiles in the second skillet, add a little water, and simmer over medium heat for 5 minutes or until the chiles are softened. Drain.

Transfer the tomato and chile mixtures to a blender. Add the ants and blend until smooth. If necessary, add a little water to loosen the mixture, taking care not to make the sauce too watery. Season with salt.

The sauce can be stored in an airtight container in the refrigerator for up to 3 days.

SINALOAN SAUCE

SALSA SINALOENSE

ï ʋ ◗ ♦ ❧ -30

Prep time: 10 minutes
Cooking time: 10 minutes
Makes: 1¼ cups (10 fl oz/300 ml)

- ¼ dried chile de árbol, stemmed
- ½ white onion, chopped
- 2 cloves garlic
- ½ tablespoon ground oregano, toasted
- ½ tablespoon black pepper, toasted
- ½ tablespoon cumin seeds, toasted
- ¼ tablespoon cloves, toasted
- ¼ cup (2 fl oz/60 ml) white vinegar
- Salt

Place the chiles in a small saucepan and add enough water to cover. Cook over medium–high heat for 10 minutes or until the chiles are softened. Drain.

In a saucepan, combine the chile, onion, and garlic. Add enough water to cover. Bring to a boil over medium–high heat and cook for 10 minutes or until the chile is softened. Drain.

Transfer the vegetables to a blender. Add the herbs and spices and vinegar and blend until smooth. Season with salt.

FRESH SALSAS

GUACAMOLE

GUACAMOLE

Prep time: 10 minutes
Makes: 1¼ cups (10 fl oz/300 ml)

- 1 serrano chile, thinly sliced into rings, with seeds
- 1 clove garlic
- ½ white onion, finely chopped
- 4 avocados, pitted and cubed
- 2 tomatoes, seeded and finely chopped
- Chopped cilantro (coriander) leaves
- Juice of 3 key limes
- Salt

In a *molcajete* or large mortar and pestle, crush the chile, garlic, and onion into a paste. Add the avocados and gently mash. Using a spoon, mix in the tomatoes, cilantro (coriander), and lime juice. Season with salt.

Serve the guacamole in the *molcajete* or mortar and pestle.

The guacamole can be stored in an airtight container in the refrigerator for up to 1 day.

PICKLED RED ONIONS

CEBOLLA MORADA ENCURTIDA

Prep time: 15 minutes
Makes: 1¼ cups (10 fl oz/300 ml)

- 4 red onions
- 2–3 tablespoons salt
- 2 habaneros, stemmed and thinly sliced
- Juice of 15 key limes
- ½ teaspoon ground oregano

Place the onions on a cutting board and, using a sharp knife, cut each in half widthwise and then thinly slice each half.

In a bowl, toss the onion with the salt. Let stand at room temperature for 10 minutes or until the onion has released its water and has softened. Drain.

Transfer the onion to a colander and rinse under running water to remove any excess salt.

Put the onion in a clean bowl. Stir in the habaneros, lime juice, and oregano.

The pickled red onions can be stored in an airtight container in the refrigerator for up to 2 days

SMOKED DRIED CHILE SALSA

K'UUT BI IK

Prep time: 5 minutes
Cooking time: 10 minutes
Makes: 1¼ cups (10 fl oz/300 ml)

- 30 dried chiles de árbol, stemmed
- Juice of 10 sour oranges
- Salt

Heat a skillet over high heat. Add the chiles and cook for 5–7 minutes, taking care not to burn them.

In a blender, blend the chiles and sour orange juice until smooth. Season with salt.

The salsa can be stored in an airtight container in the refrigerator for up to 3 days.

PICO DE GALLO

PICO DE GALLO

Prep time: 5 minutes
Makes: 1¼ cups (10 fl oz/300 ml)

- 20 cilantro (coriander) leaves, finely chopped
- 10 tomatoes, finely chopped
- 2 serrano chiles, stemmed and finely chopped
- 1 white onion, finely chopped
- Pinch of salt
- Juice of 1 key lime

This sauce is quick to make, and you'll need only a cutting board, a sharp knife, and a deep bowl. If you like, remove the tomato seeds to avoid excess liquid.

Combine all the ingredients in a bowl.

The pico de gallo can be stored in an airtight container in the refrigerator for up to 1 day.

RAW SALSA VERDE

SALSA VERDE CRUDA

Prep time: 10 minutes
Makes: 1¼ cups (10 fl oz/300 ml)

- 10 green tomatoes
- 1 serrano chile
- ½ white onion, chopped
- 20 cilantro (coriander) leaves
- Juice of 2 key limes
- Salt

Put all the ingredients in a blender and blend until smooth, about 5 minutes. Season with salt and lime juice.

The salsa can be stored in an airtight container in the refrigerator for up to 2 days.

TAMULADA SAUCE

¨ⅴ◗◆☙ -5 -30

Prep time: 5 minutes
Makes: 1¼ cups (10 fl oz/300 ml)

- 20 habanero chiles, stemmed
- ¼ teaspoon salt, plus extra to season
- Juice of 10 oranges
- ¼ cup (2 fl oz/60 ml) white vinegar
- ¼ teaspoon sugar

Using a *molcajete* or mortar and pestle, crush the chiles and salt into a paste.

Transfer to a bowl and stir in the orange juice. Season with vinegar, salt and a little sugar.

The sauce can be stored in an airtight container in the refrigerator for up to 3 days.

PEBRE SAUCE

¨ⅴ◗◆☙ -30

Prep time: 5 minutes
Makes: Scant 1 cup (7 fl oz/200 ml)

- 2 tomatoes, finely chopped
- ½ white onion, finely chopped
- 3 fresh chiles, such as serrano, jalapeño, or habanero, seeded, deveined, and finely chopped (optional)
- 2 cups (1 oz/35 g) finely chopped cilantro (coriander) leaves
- White wine vinegar, to season
- ¼ teaspoon salt

In a bowl, mix together the tomato, onion, chiles, and cilantro (coriander). Season with vinegar and salt, then stir to form a moist paste.

The salsa can be stored in an airtight container in the refrigerator for up to 3 days.

BOILED/ CHARRED SALSAS

CHARRED RED SALSA

SALSA ROJA MOLCAJETEADA

🌶 𝓋 ◗ ◖ ❧ -5 -30

Prep time: 15 minutes
Cooking time: 10 minutes
Makes: 1¼ cups (10 fl oz/300 ml)

- 5 large tomatoes, halved
- 2 cloves garlic
- 2 red serrano chiles, stemmed
- ½ white onion, chopped
- Salt

Heat a small grill (griddle) or skillet over medium–high heat for 5 minutes.

Add all the ingredients except the salt. Cook for 10 minutes, turning constantly, until browned on all sides. Transfer the garlic and chiles to a plate if they char more quickly than the tomatoes and onion.

Using a *molcajete* or mortar and pestle, mash the garlic into a paste, then the chiles, onion, and tomatoes, mashing after adding each to the garlic. (You can mash the onion and tomatoes less thoroughly.) Season with salt.

The salsa can be stored in an airtight container in the refrigerator for up to 2 days.

CHARRED GREEN SALSA

SALSA VERDE MOLCAJETEADA

🌶 𝓋 ◗ ◖ ❧ -5 -30

Prep time: 15 minutes
Cooking time: 10 minutes
Makes: 1¼ cups (10 fl oz/300 ml)

- 7 green tomatoes, halved
- ½ white onion, chopped
- 2 cloves garlic
- 1 green serrano chile, stemmed
- Salt

Heat a small grill (griddle) or skillet over medium–high heat for 5 minutes.

Add all the ingredients except the salt. Cook for 10 minutes, turning constantly, until browned. Transfer the garlic and chile to a plate if they char more quickly than the tomatoes and onion.

Using a *molcajete* or mortar and pestle, mash the garlic into a paste, then the chiles, onion, and tomatoes, mashing after adding each to the garlic. (You can mash the onion and tomatoes less thoroughly.) Season with salt.

The salsa can be stored in an airtight container in the refrigerator for up to 2 days.

RED MORITA SALSA

SALSA ROJA CON CHILE MORITA

🌶 ᐯ ◖ ◉ ❦

Prep time: 20 minutes
Cooking time: 25 minutes
Makes: 1¼ cups (10 fl oz/300 ml)

• 15 guajillo chiles, seeded and deveined
• 5 large tomatoes, skin removed
• 2 cloves garlic
• ½ white onion, chopped
• 2 tablespoons olive oil
• Salt

Put the chiles, tomatoes, garlic, and onion in a saucepan. Add enough water to cover. Bring to a boil over medium–high heat and cook for 15 minutes or until the chiles are softened. Drain.

Transfer the tomato mixture to a blender and blend until smooth. If necessary, add a little water to loosen the mixture.

Heat the oil in a skillet over medium heat. Pour in the chile mixture and stir constantly for 10 minutes or until the sauce darkens and thickens. Remove from the heat and season with salt.

The salsa can be stored in an airtight container in the refrigerator for up to 2 days.

GREEN SERRANO SALSA

SALSA VERDE HERVIDA CON SERRANO

🌶 ᐯ ◖ ◉ ❦ -30

Prep time: 10 minutes
Cooking time: 15 minutes
Makes: 1¼ cups (10 fl oz/300 ml)

• 7 large green tomatoes, halved
• ½ white onion, chopped
• 2 cloves garlic
• 2 green serrano chiles, stemmed
• 6–7 sprigs cilantro (coriander)
• ¼ teaspoon ground cumin, toasted
• 1 tablespoon olive oil
• ¼ teaspoon salt

Put the tomatoes, onion, garlic, and chiles in a saucepan. Add enough water to cover. Bring to a boil over medium–high heat. Cook for 10 minutes or until the tomatoes are very light in color. Drain, reserving the cooking liquid.

Transfer the tomato mixture to a blender, then add the cilantro (coriander) and cumin. Pulse the mixture until the cilantro is completely incorporated, adding a little cooking liquid to loosen, if necessary.

Heat the oil in a skillet over medium heat. Add the vegetable mixture and, stirring constantly to prevent it from burning, cook for 5 minutes or until the salsa is a dark green color. Remove from the heat and season with salt.

The salsa can be stored in an airtight container in the refrigerator for 3 days.

RED SERRANO SALSA

SALSA ROJA HERVIDA CON SERRANO

☉ ᵛ ◖ ◕ ❦ -30

Prep time: 10 minutes
Cooking time: 20 minutes
Makes: 1¼ cups (10 fl oz/300 ml)

- 7 tomatoes, halved
- ½ white onion, chopped
- 2 cloves garlic
- 2 serrano chiles, stemmed
- 1 tablespoon olive oil
- Salt

In a saucepan, combine the tomatoes, onion, garlic, and chiles. Add enough water to cover. Cook over medium–high heat for 10 minutes or until the chiles are softened. Drain, reserving the cooking liquid.

Transfer the tomato mixture to a blender. Blend until smooth, adding a little cooking liquid to loosen, if necessary.

Heat the oil in a skillet over medium heat. Add the vegetable mixture and, stirring constantly to prevent burning, cook for 10 minutes or until the salsa is a dark red color. Remove from the heat and season with salt.

The salsa can be stored in an airtight container in the refrigerator for up to 2 days.

GREEN TOMATO-PASILLA SALSA

SALSA DE CHILE PASILLA CON TOMATE VERDE

☉ ᵛ ◖ ◕ ❦ -30

Prep time: 10 minutes
Cooking time: 20 minutes
Makes: 1¼ cups (10 fl oz/300 ml)

- 7 large green tomatoes, halved
- ½ white onion, chopped
- 2 cloves garlic
- 15 pasilla chiles, seeded and deveined
- Pinch of ground cumin, toasted
- 1 tablespoon olive oil
- ¼ teaspoon salt

In a saucepan, combine the tomatoes, onion, garlic, and chiles. Add enough water to cover. Cook over medium–high heat for 10 minutes or until the chiles are softened. Drain.

Transfer the tomato mixture to a blender. Add the cumin and a little regular water and blend until smooth.

Heat the oil in a skillet over medium heat. Add the vegetable mixture and, stirring constantly to prevent burning, cook for 10 minutes or until the salsa is a dark brown color. Remove from the heat and season well with salt.

The salsa can be stored in an airtight container in the refrigerator for up to 2 days.

SWEET CHIPOTLE SAUCE

SALSA DE CHIPOTLE DULCE

Prep time: 10 minutes
Cooking time: 30 minutes
Makes: 1¼ cups (10 fl oz/300 ml)

- 2 cones piloncillo (10½ oz/300 g total)
- 3 large white onions, diced
- 7 cloves garlic
- 5 guajillo chiles, seeded and deveined
- 10 dried chipotle chiles, stemmed
- Scant 1 cup (7 fl oz/200 ml) white wine vinegar
- ¼ teaspoon salt

In a saucepan, combine the piloncillo, onions, garlic, chiles, and vinegar. Pour in 2½ cups (20 fl oz/600 ml) of water. Cook over medium–high heat for 20 minutes, until the chiles are softened. Drain, retaining some of the cooking liquid.

Transfer the mixture to a blender and blend well. If necessary, add a little cooking water to loosen the mixture. Pour the mixture back into the saucepan. Simmer over medium heat for 10 minutes or until the sauce thickens, stirring constantly to prevent burning. Remove from the heat and season with the salt.

The sauce can be stored in an airtight container in the refrigerator for up to 3 days.

DRIED CHILE SAUCE

SALSA DE CHILES SECOS

Prep time: 10 minutes
Cooking time: 30 minutes
Makes: 1¼ cups (10 fl oz/300 ml)

- 6 tomatoes, halved
- ½ white onion, chopped
- 2 cloves garlic
- 8 ancho chiles, seeded and deveined
- 8 pasilla chiles, seeded and deveined
- 4 dried chiles de árbol, stemmed
- 1 tablespoon olive oil
- Salt

Heat a grill (griddle) or skillet over medium–high heat for 5 minutes. Add the tomatoes, onion, and garlic and cook, turning them occasionally, for 15 minutes or until a dark brown color.

Fill a small saucepan halfway with water. Add the chiles and bring to a boil over high heat. Boil for 7 minutes or until the chiles are softened. Drain.

Transfer the tomato mixture and chiles to a blender and blend until smooth. If necessary, add a little water to loosen the mixture.

Heat the oil in a skillet over medium–high heat. Add the tomato-chile mixture and, stirring constantly to prevent burning, cook for 5 minutes. Remove from the heat and season with salt.

The sauce can be stored in an airtight container in the refrigerator for up to 1 week.

MANZANO CHILE TOMATO SAUCE

SALSA DE CHILE MANZANO CON TOMATE AMARILLO

ï ν ◕ ◌ ✿ -30

Prep time: 10 minutes
Cooking time: 20 minutes
Makes: 1¼ cups (10 fl oz/300 ml)

- 4 tablespoons olive oil, divided
- ½ white onion, chopped
- 2 cloves garlic
- 8 yellow tomatoes, halved
- 3 fresh manzano chiles, seeded and deveined
- Salt

Heat 3 tablespoons of the olive oil in a skillet over medium–high heat. Add the onion and garlic, and sauté for 5 minutes or until the onion is golden. Add the tomatoes and chiles, stirring constantly for 10 minutes or until the tomatoes begin to release their juices. Add enough water to cover the ingredients halfway. Bring to a boil, then remove from the heat.

Transfer the mixture to a blender and blend until smooth.

Heat the remaining 1 tablespoon of oil in the skillet over low heat. Pour in the tomato-chile mixture and increase the heat to medium–high. Bring the mixture to a boil, stirring constantly to prevent the sauce from burning. Remove from the heat and season with salt.

The sauce can be stored in an airtight container in the refrigerator for up to 2 days.

CORN TORTILLAS

TORTILLAS DE MAÍZ (HARINA DE MAÍZ)

Prep time: 15 minutes
Cooking time: 5 minutes
Makes: 30

- 2 lb 4 oz/1 kg cornmeal
- Pinch of salt
- Generous 2 cups (17 fl oz/500 ml) warm water
- Cornflour, for dusting

In a deep bowl, mix together the cornmeal and salt. Create a well in the center of the mixture and gradually add the water while mixing with your hands. Once all the water has been incorporated, transfer the dough to a surface lightly dusted with corn flour.

Knead the dough with the palm of your hands, spreading it out and then bringing it back together. Knead for 10 minutes.

Portion and, using the palms of your hand, roll the dough into 30 golf ball–size balls. (For the large tortillas used in the flautas recipes, spread the dough in a cylinder-shape ball.)

Place a ball of dough between 2 pieces of plastic wrap (clingfilm). Using a tortilla press or rolling pin, press on the ball with just enough force to flatten the tortilla. Peel the plastic wrap off the tortilla.

Heat a skillet over medium heat. Place a tortilla in the skillet. When the edges of the tortilla begin to peel away from the pan, flip it over. Cook the tortilla until the edges again begin to peel away from the pan. Flip it again, and when it inflates, remove from the pan.

Repeat the process with the remaining dough.

NIXTAMALIZED CORN TORTILLAS

TORTILLA DE MAÍZ NIXTAMALIZADO

Prep time: 1 hour
Cooking time: 30 minutes
Makes: 25

- 2 lb 4 oz/1 kg yellow corn kernels
- 1 teaspoon (⅓ oz/11 g) quicklime

In a deep bowl filled with water, wash the corn to remove any impurities.

Put the quicklime in a metal container and pour ½ cup (4 fl oz/120 ml) of water over the top to activate it. This is a chemical process, so be careful, as the mixture will become hot.

Put the washed corn in a large saucepan, add enough water to cover, then stir in the lime mixture. Cook over high heat for 20 minutes or until the corn is tender and the husks are soft enough to be removed by hand. Drain, then wash the corn thoroughly with water, removing all the corn husks.

Using a food mill, grind the corn into a smooth paste, adding water as needed to facilitate the grinding and prevent the dough from drying out.

Portion and, using the palms of your hand, roll the dough into 25 golf ball–size balls. (For the large tortillas used in the flautas recipes, spread the dough in a cylinder-shape ball.) Place a ball of dough between 2 pieces of plastic wrap (clingfilm). Using a tortilla press or rolling pin, press on the ball with just enough force to flatten the tortilla. Peel the plastic wrap off the tortilla.

Heat a skillet over medium heat. Place a tortilla in the skillet. When the edges of the tortilla begin to peel away from the pan, flip it over. Cook the tortilla until the edges again begin to peel away from the pan. Flip it again, and when it inflates, remove it from the pan.

Repeat the process with the remaining dough.

TORTILLAS

FLOUR TORTILLAS

Prep time: 20 minutes, plus 30 minutes resting time
Makes: 30

- 4 lb/1.8 kg all-purpose (plain) flour
- ⅔ oz/18 g baking powder
- ⅔ oz/18 g salt
- 12¾ cups (3 quarts/3 liters) milk
- 19 oz/540 g butter

Put the flour, baking powder, and salt in the bowl of a stand mixer. Pour in the milk.

Mix at medium speed for 20 minutes or until the gluten develops in the dough. To test this, take a small portion of the dough and, with your fingertips, spread it out to create an elastic film. If the film doesn't break, the dough is ready. If it does break, mix the dough 1–2 minutes longer, then test it again.

Once the dough is ready, add a third of the butter with the mixer on medium speed, mixing until incorporated. Repeat the process two more times until all the butter has been incorporated.

Remove the dough from the mixer and let it rest in a dry place, covered with a clean kitchen towel, for 30 minutes.

Portion and, using the palms of your hand, roll the dough into 30 golf ball-size balls.

Place a ball of dough between 2 pieces of plastic wrap (clingfilm). Using a tortilla press or rolling pin, press on the ball with just enough force to flatten the tortilla. Peel the plastic wrap off the tortilla.

Heat a skillet over medium heat. Place a tortilla in the skillet. When the edges of the tortilla begin to peel away from the pan, flip it over. Cook the tortilla until the edges again begin to peel away from the pan. Flip it again, and when it inflates, remove it from the pan.

Repeat the process with the remaining dough.

GLOSSARY

ACHIOTE OR AXIOTE

A fruit of the Americas. The paste made with it in the southeast of Mexico is called red recado and is the base of pibil dishes—those wrapped in banana leaves and baked underground. The seeds are used to make red food coloring.

AYOCOTE

A large bean—in fact, the largest that exists in Mexico. The beans measure more than ¾ inches/2 cm long and vary in color depending on the region. They can be purple, black, brown, white, or mottled, but, when cooked, almost all of them lose their original color and take on a dark brown tone. The red flowers of the plant are also edible.

CHAPULÍN

An acidic grasshopper found in the states of Oaxaca, Mexico, and Guerrero. They're sold in various sizes; the smaller ones are milder in flavor. To prepare, they're washed and boiled in salted water, then toasted and eaten with chili sauce, with garlic mojo, or simply with salt and lemon, as well as in many other delicious ways. They can be used as a substitution for meat for tacos.

CHICATANA

A species of large ant with a dark brown or reddish color. It is one of the most abundant in Mexico. The workers are known as arrieras, and the others, whether males or females, are known as chicatanas. They build their anthills in clay soils, and are abundant in the months of May, June, and July. Depending on the region, they are known by different names: sakol, say, xulab, cicateras, talaras, leaf-cutters, big-headed ants, and parasol ants, among others. When captured, they are placed in clay pots with water and then toasted to prevent decomposition. Their heads and legs must be removed and discarded before eating.

CHICHILO

A mole of Oaxacan origin, also known as black chichilo. Despite being the least known, it is considered one of the seven famous moles of Oaxaca. The color of the chichilo is thanks to the mixture of toasted chiles—chilhuacle negro, pasilla, mulato—and burnt tortillas, which also give it a smoky flavor.

CHINTEXTLE

A ground chili paste of which there are many varieties; almost all include ground Mixe chile. This sauce, which is usually eaten with tortillas, can be made from only water and ground chile, or you can make it with dried shrimp, garlic, oil and vinegar, pumpkin seeds, walnuts, almonds, or black beans.

CHIRIVÍA

A root (Pastinaca sativa) used as a vegetable. Its cultivation dates back centuries to Eurasia. It is similar to carrot though white in color and with an anise flavor. The flavor improves after a frost, since the cold converts part of the starch into sugar.

ESCAMOLES

Eggs, larvae, and pupae of black or red ants, similar in appearance to puffed rice. They are found only during the months of March and April.

MACHACA

Typically from the north of Mexico, this type of beef—generally from the loin—is prepared using a process of salting and drying in the sun before being pounded. Its name comes from the process of crushing it with a stone or stick, rather than grinding it or cutting it into small pieces (machaca means "pounder" or "crusher").

MAGUEY

The maguey is a type of agave that grows approximately 5 feet/1.5 meters tall but with a short stem. The succulent's leaves are known as stalks and sprout from the stem in a rosette shape. They can be light green in color, sometimes tinged with yellow, and are thick and fleshy, with spines at the edges.

MISO

A condiment made from soybeans; a cereal such as rice, wheat, or barley; and sea salt; and fermented with koji mold. Depending on the degree of fermentation, the flavor of this paste varies from sweet to salty, and its color from yellow to dark brown.

NIXTAMALIZATION

The process by which corn is cooked by bringing it to a boil with quick-lime or ground lime, during which a chemical reaction occurs that generates heat, helping soften and loosen the corn husk. Thanks to this chemical reaction, the particles inside the grain stick together during grinding. This is because, upon absorbing water, the starches pass into a plastic or gel state. Nixta-malization makes corn proteins more digestible, and brings out the niacin found in the grain, which helps prevent diseases such as pellagra.

SIKIL PAK

A thick sauce, traditionally from the Yucatán Peninsula, prepared with pumpkin seeds, tomato, habanero chile, cilantro (coriander), chives, garlic, and salt. It is spread on toast and eaten as a snack.

YUZU

A citrus fruit native to China but grown mainly in Japan. Its pulp is bitter and full of seeds. It has a flavor similar to that of grapefruit. It is used to make an infusion or in jams and desserts, and replaces lemon in some traditional Japanese dishes. Its juice is used to make ponzu, a traditional sauce in Japanese cuisine.

YUZU KOSHO

A condiment made of chile, salt, and yuzu peel and juice. It is native to the island of Kyushu, one of Japan's southern islands. Yuzu kosho comes in both red and green versions, depending on the color of the chiles used in its preparation. It is very fragrant, and its flavor is spicy and slightly acidic.

INDEX

A - B

B - C

C - D

D - F

F - L

L - N

P - T

T - V

V - Y

AUTHOR'S ACKNOWLEDGMENTS

I would like to thank the following people on my team for their invaluable help in making this book possible: Alonso, Araceli, Axel, Bruno, Gio, Gonzalo, Israel, Jochs, Liz, and Pati.

I would also like to thank the Phaidon team: publisher Deb Aaronson, creative director Julia Hasting, project editor Michelle Meade, culinary managing editor Ellie Smith, and executive commissioning editor Emily Takoudes.

BIOGRAPHIES

ENRIQUE OLVERA

Enrique Olvera, a Mexico City native and Culinary Institute of America graduate, opened Pujol in 2000. Pujol is a cornerstone of Mexican cuisine, emphasizing Mexican heritage and celebrating heirloom seasonal ingredients. It was awarded two Michelin stars, is a part of the Relais & Châteaux family, and consistently ranks on The World's 50 Best Restaurants list.

Olvera expanded to the United States with Cosme in New York, followed by Atla. He also opened Eno in Mexico City, co-owns Criollo in Oaxaca, and served as the creative chef for Manta in Los Cabos. In 2018, he launched Casa Teo, a creative residency space and Molino "El Pujol," promoting native corn varieties. He further expanded with the Ticuchi bar in Mexico City, exploring agave spirits; Damian and Ditroit in Los Angeles; and Carao in Riviera Nayarit.

In 2024, Olvera opened Esse Taco in Brooklyn. He has also been featured extensively in the media, including documentaries and Netflix's *Chef's Table*. He has authored several books, including *Mexico from the Inside Out* and *Tu Casa Mi Casa* with Phaidon.

Olvera is a strong advocate for Mexican cuisine, both domestically and internationally. This has had a profound influence on the Mexican gastronomic scene, with Pujol alumni heading several of the country's most prestigious restaurants.

ALONSO RUVALCABA

Alonso Ruvalcaba is a taco-obsessed Mexican food critic, who has written about tacos for major publications, including the *Los Angeles Times*, *Bon Appetit*, and *Vice*.

RECIPE NOTES

Butter is salted butter, unless otherwise specified.

Eggs are US size large (UK size medium), unless otherwise specified. Herbs are fresh, unless otherwise specified.

Milk is full-fat (whole) or reduced-fat (semi-skimmed) milk, unless otherwise specified.

Olives can be pitted or unpitted, unless otherwise specified.

Pepper is freshly ground black pepper, unless otherwise specified.

Salt is fine sea salt, unless otherwise specified.

Sugar is white granulated or table sugar, unless otherwise specified.

Individual vegetables and fruits, such as carrots and apples, are assumed to be medium, unless otherwise specified, and should be peeled and/or washed unless otherwise specified.

Where neutral oil is specified, use vegetable, canola (rapeseed), grapeseed, sunflower, corn, or light olive oil.

Cup, imperial, and metric measurements are used in this book. Follow one set of measurements throughout, not a mixture, as they are not interchangeable.

All tablespoon and teaspoon measurements given are level, not heaping, unless otherwise specified.

1 teaspoon = 5 ml; 1 tablespoon = 15 ml. Australian standard tablespoons are 20 ml, so Australian readers are advised to use 3 teaspoons in place of 1 tablespoon when measuring small quantities.

When no quantity is specified, for example of oils, salts, and herbs used for finishing dishes or for deep-frying, quantities are discretionary and flexible.

Cooking and preparation times are for guidance only. If using a convection (fan) oven, follow the manufacturer's directions concerning oven temperatures.

When deep-frying, heat the oil to the temperature specified, or until a cube of bread browns in 30 seconds. After frying, drain fried foods on paper towels.

When sterilizing jars for preserves, wash the jars in clean, hot water and rinse thoroughly. Heat the oven to 275°F/140°C/Gas Mark 1. Place the jars on a baking sheet and place in the oven to dry.

Exercise a high level of caution when following recipes involving any potentially hazardous activity, including the use of high temperatures and open flames and when deep-frying.

In particular, when deep-frying, add food carefully to avoid splashing, wear long sleeves, and never leave the pan unattended.

Some recipes include raw or very lightly cooked eggs, meat, or fish, and fermented products. These should be avoided by the elderly, infants, pregnant women, convalescents, and anyone with an impaired immune system.

All herbs, shoots, flowers, and leaves should be picked fresh from a clean source.

Do exercise caution when foraging for ingredients, which should only be eaten if an expert has deemed them safe to eat. In particular, do not gather wild mushrooms yourself before seeking the advice of an expert who has confirmed their suitability for human consumption.

As some species of mushrooms have been known to cause allergic reaction and illness, do take extra care when cooking and eating mushrooms and do seek immediate medical help if you experience a reaction after preparing or eating them.

REFERENCES

Ricardo Muñoz Zurita, *Diccionario enciclopédico de la gastronomía mexicana*. Larousse, 2012.

Enrique Olvera, *En la milpa*. 1st edition, 2011.

Enrique Olvera, *Mexico from the Inside Out*. 1st edition, Phaidon, 2015.

Enrique Olvera, *Pujol Veinte*. 1st edition, 2020.

Enrique Olvera, *Tu Casa Mi Casa*. 1st edition, Phaidon, 2019.